Mealtime Magic:

Delicious Dinners In Half The Time

Mealtime Magic:
Delicious Dinners In Half The Time

by

Amy Houts

Houts & Home Publications LLC

Maryville, Missouri

Mealtime Magic: Delicious Dinners in Half the Time

Cover design: Megg Houts
Interior layout design: Megg Houts

© 2013 Amy Houts, Houts & Home Publications LLC
All rights reserved. No part of this document may be reproduced, stored in retrieval systems, or transmitted in any form or by any means, electronic, mechanical, photocopying, recording, or otherwise, without prior written permission of Houts & Home Publications LLC.

Printed in the United States of America
ISBN 978-0-9855084-0-1

For inquiries contact:
Amy Houts, President, Houts & Home Publications LLC
Telephone: 660.562.3122
E-mail: amyonline@amyhouts.com
Website: www.houtsandhome.com

Library of Congress Control Number: 2012918307

Table of Contents

Delicious Dinners with Chicken
Chapter 1: Chicken Breasts 12
Chapter 2: Whole Chickens 32

Delicious Dinners with Turkey
Chapter 3: Whole Turkeys 50
Chapter 4: Ground Turkey 63
Chapter 5: Ground Turkey and Ground Beef Blend 67

Delicious Dinners with Beef
Chapter 6: Ground Beef 71
Chapter 7: Beef Stews .99
Chapter 8: Beef Steaks 104
Chapter 9: Beef Roasts 112

Delicious Dinners with Pork
Chapter 10: Pork Sausage 125
Chapter 11: Pork Chops 137
Chapter 12: Pork Roasts 142
Chapter 13: Ham 152

Delicious Dinners with Fish and Seafood
Chapter 14: Fish and Seafood 170

Delicious Meatless Dinners
Chapter 15: Meatless Soups, Stews, and Casseroles 186

Plans 194
Index 198

Introduction

No More Boring Leftovers

Leftovers are boring. So what can you do with the rest of that beef roast, those chicken legs, that ham steak? Try a little magic: Mealtime Magic! How does it work? Main dish recipes in this cookbook follow a three-day schedule. Part of one meal is used in a second and third meal. Each is totally different from the others, so your family will not think they are eating leftovers. Yes, you can make leftovers interesting while saving yourself time, energy, and money!

Using this three-day method, you don't need to start from scratch each night. Meal planning will follow a natural flow. You won't have to decide what to eat for dinner. Even though all meals are homemade, you'll be spending less time cooking, and that will give you more time to do the things you really want to do. You'll even have fewer pots and pans to wash.

For example, one evening, you bake chicken breasts in a spicy tomato sauce and serve it over rice. The next night, dice chicken to create chicken chili with barley. The following night, shred the remaining baked chicken breasts to make cheesy chicken enchiladas. Don't feel like spicy food? Begin with slow-cooked French dip sandwiches. Follow up with beef-vegetable soup. The third day? How about quick and easy beef pot pie?

I've been cooking this way for years, and it's the best way I know to serve satisfying, nutritious meals to my family in the most efficient, time-saving way. With work, family, school, and other commitments, scheduling time to cook and eat a meal together can be a challenge. That's why I created Mealtime Magic: Delicious Dinners in Half the Time—to make your life easier.

Saving Money

Using this helpful method, you will save money. Americans throw away tons of leftovers equaling millions of dollars. According to a 2012 article titled, "Your Scraps Add Up: Reducing food waste can save money and resources," by the Natural Resources Defense Council, "The average American throws away between $28-$43 in the form of about 20 pounds of food each month." See: http://www.nrdc.org/living/eatingwell/files/foodwaste_2pgr.pdf

You will save hundreds of dollars each year by creating dishes with leftovers that you and your family enjoy. Besides throwing away fewer leftovers, you will save money by eating at home more and eating out less. After all, part of your meal is already cooked. The hard part is over. All you need to do is add to what you already have.

Pleasing Picky Eaters

Research shows that picky eaters are the biggest challenge at mealtime. The majority of these recipes have been tested on our two daughters while they were growing up. They challenged me to create delicious main dishes that have been requested again and again. I began cooking for my family when I was 12 and attended the Culinary Institute of America in New York after graduating from high school. This foundation in cooking has served me well over the past 40 years. My expertise in creating recipes that my family loves motivated me to share my knowledge with you. I hope you enjoy the recipes I've included, which represent good, home cooking from the heartland of the USA. Recipes use basic ingredients that you probably have in your pantry or can easily find in the grocery store.

Healthy Alternatives

Eating at home is healthier, too, because you know the ingredients you are using. You can cook with natural chicken, lean cuts of beef, and fresh vegetables. To create low-fat, low-cholesterol meals, mix ground beef and ground turkey, or substitute ground turkey for ground beef. Choose healthier cooking methods. Rather than deep-fat frying chicken, you can bake it, creating a low-fat alternative. Use brown rice instead of white rice. Flavor food with herbs and spices to cut down on salt. Plan to alternate foods high in cholesterol, such as beef, sausage, and shellfish, with foods lower in cholesterol, such as chicken, turkey, and fish. Controlling portion sizes so that you feel satisfied, but don't overeat, is another healthy advantage of cooking at home. *Come eat, enjoy, and relax in the comfort of your own home.*

Coordinated Side Dishes

The focus of this book is on main dishes. Simple suggestions for side dishes are included to complete your meal.

See www.houtsandhome.com for recipes for side dishes and more.

Guidelines for Safe Leftovers

The United States Department of Agriculture (USDA) states that cooked meat is safe to keep in the refrigerator for three to four days. For fish and seafood, only two days. The fish and seafood chapter of this cookbook follows a two-day schedule rather than a three-day schedule like the meat chapters. While it's usually safe to keep meatless dishes for more than two days, the meatless chapter follows a two-day schedule as well.

Alternating Foods

Some allergists recommend alternating foods instead of eating the same type of meat three days in a row. You can alternate between two basic meats for nearly a week's worth of dinners. For example, start with an herb-roasted chicken on day one. Follow with a savory beef stew on day two, chicken-pecan salad on day three, and easy beef and noodles on day four. However, if you follow this alternating plan, you will exceed the USDA guidelines of keeping cooked meat in the refrigerator more than four days. So for safety reasons freeze a portion of the remaining meat in the three-day cycle. For better taste and consistency when defrosted, when you freeze ground beef, turkey, or pork, mix in chopped tomatoes or broth, something to keep it moist, before freezing.

Meal Plan

Plan to make meals that cook several hours, such as roasts or stews, on the weekend when you have more time. Scan through ingredients for all three recipes to see what you need to buy at the store. Other items might be staples that you keep stocked in your pantry and refrigerator. Once you begin using this book, you'll find that you will start stocking your kitchen with frozen or pantry items you often use so you'll be ready for a three-day plan without going to the grocery store. I nearly always have fresh carrots and celery in the refrigerator, frozen noodles in my deep freeze, and chicken soup base and dried parsley in the cabinet. When I have cooked chicken, I have everything I need for a pot of savory chicken and noodles, a family favorite.

Serving Sizes

Most meals in this book yield four servings. They have served my family of four—my husband, our two daughters, and me—over many years as the girls grew up. Depending on the ages and appetites of the people in your family, you might need to adjust the amount of meat in your basic recipe.

Why Mealtime Magic Works

You'll be surprised that one chicken breast can feed two to four people; once it is sliced and cubed, it seems like more than one little chicken breast. It reminds me of Piaget's theory of cognitive development in children younger than age seven or eight, whose skewed belief of an object magically becoming <u>more</u> just because it's in pieces—a slice of cheese becomes <u>more</u> when it's cut into pieces. In a similar way, you would psychologically never be satisfied with eating a fourth of a chicken breast, but diced in a soup, it's the perfect amount with the addition of fresh veggies or dried beans. It not only seems like more, but is more than enough for a filling, satisfying meal after adding vegetables and grains.

Purchasing Beef, Pork, Fish, and Chicken

A related issue is the size and weight of the cut of meat in a recipe. When meat is the main dish, allow one-fourth pound per adult for boneless beef, pork, or fish. To increase recipe yield, consider that one pound of ground beef feeds a family of four, so if you have six people to feed, you will need to multiply the ingredients in the recipe by one and a half.

Like beef, pork, and fish, a pound of boneless chicken breasts yields four servings. However, while the average chicken breasts are four ounces (one-fourth pound), they range from small to large, so plan by weight, not by quantity. You might need to cut a large chicken breast in two. When buying a whole chicken, choose a meatier broiler-fryer, roaster, or stewing hen, even if it costs a bit more. A chicken that costs more also has more meat in relation to the bones. Plan a whole pound per adult for a meal where bone-in chicken is the main dish (a four-pound chicken for a family of four). The basic recipes for each two- or three-day plan will call for more than these amounts, since some of the meat is reserved for subsequent meals.

Substitutions

You can switch some of the recipes around, as long as you keep the following guidelines in mind. Note that each basic recipe and additional recipes are best when cooked a specific way: sautéed, stewed, grilled, roasted, etc. Sometimes you can substitute, for example, baked chicken for stewed, but keep in mind that when stewed, the texture is soft and moist, while baked is more dense and dry. Grilled chicken has a strong grilled flavor that pairs well with BBQ sauce and stir fry, but is not good with milder dishes such as chicken and noodles. Chicken cooked with a spicy tomato-pepper sauce is best for spicy dishes like chili and enchiladas.

Create Your Own

Do you have some family favorites you don't see in this book? Create your own three-day plan using a basic recipe and expanding the list to include great dinners you and your family love. That's why I've included some fill-in-the-blanks at the end of each section. This book is meant to be for you—so make a few of your own custom plans. Making your life easier and more enjoyable—that's the goal of Houts & Home Publications LLC.

Amy Houts, Author

Mealtime Magic: Delicious Dinners in Half the Time

President and Publisher, Houts & Home Publications LLC

Delicious Dinners with Chicken

Chapter 1: Chicken Breasts

Defrosting Chicken Breasts

If chicken breasts are frozen, defrost completely before you begin cooking. The best way to defrost chicken is in the refrigerator where it takes at least a day or 2. If you defrost chicken on the counter, submerge it in a bowl of cold water and check every half hour. If the water is not cold, dump, and add cold water to the bowl. Once the chicken is defrosted, refrigerate until ready to cook. When Defrosting chicken in the microwave, cook it right away.

Remove Skin

Often the skin on boneless chicken breasts has been removed before you purchase them. If not, use paper towels to help grab and pull off the chicken skin. Discard skin. Then the chicken breasts are ready to cook.

Remove Tendon

Sometimes a boned chicken breast comes with a fillet on the underside of the breast. Sometimes the fillets are removed before packaging the chicken breast and sold separately as "chicken tenders" for breading or for stir-fry. In order for the fillet to be tender, you need to remove the white tendon. With a chef's knife, carefully cut and tug on the tendon to remove it. Discard tendon.

For more on information about chicken, see the United States Department of Agriculture (USDA) link: http://www.fsis.usda.gov/fact_sheets/chicken_from_farm_to_table/index.asp

Three-Day Plan

Day 1: Asian Chicken Salad ⟶ **Day 2:** Creamy Chicken Alfredo ⟶ **Day 3:** Rainy Day Chicken-Rice Soup

Asian Chicken Salad

6 boneless, skinless chicken breasts
1 quart chicken broth
OR 1 quart water and 4 teaspoons chicken soup base
¼ cup sugar
1 cup sliced almonds
1 head romaine lettuce
1 (11-oz.) can Mandarin oranges

Dressing:
¼ cup oil
2 tablespoons cider vinegar
2 tablespoons sugar
½ teaspoon salt
1 tablespoon chopped fresh parsley
OR 1 teaspoon dried parsley

Place chicken breasts in a large (6 - 8 quart) pot. Add chicken broth or water and soup base. Bring to a boil over high heat. Turn down heat to medium-low. Depending on the size, simmer chicken breasts for 20 to 30 minutes until cooked through. Remove chicken from broth and let rest 10 minutes in order to retain juices. Pour chicken broth into a container; reserve in the refrigerate to use in the next two meals. Slice 2 chicken breasts lengthwise and crosswise to dice. Place diced chicken in a serving bowl. Reserve remaining chicken breasts for the next two meals.

Place a sheet of waxed paper on a cookie sheet; set aside. To prepare candied almonds, pour ¼ cup sugar into a small skillet. Melt sugar over low heat, which takes 5 - 10 minutes. Watch closely; sugar can burn. As soon as the sugar dissolves into a light brown liquid, quickly add almonds and carefully stir with a metal spatula (plastic will melt). Note: melted sugar is very hot! Pour candied almonds onto the waxed paper lined cookie sheet using the spatula to scrape the pan if needed. When cool, crumble and place in a serving bowl.

Using a large serrated knife, cut Romaine lettuce into approximately 1-inch widths on a cutting board. Place lettuce in a large bowl and cover with cold water. Use your hand to stir the lettuce so dirt and sand can fall to the bottom. Gather the lettuce, carrying it up out of the water and into a salad spinner basket. Rotate to dry (or pat dry with towels). Place in a serving bowl. Drain oranges; place in a serving bowl.

For fresh parsley, place a small bunch in a colander and rinse under cold water. Rub the parsley with your fingers to remove dirt. Shake off excess water. Pat dry with a paper towel. Hold the parsley in a bunch and cut the leaves from the stems. Discard stems. Place leaves in a bowl and snip with kitchen shears or use a knife to chop on a cutting board.

For dressing, mix oil, vinegar, sugar, salt, and fresh or dried parsley in a measuring cup. Beat with a wire whisk or blend in a shaker bottle. Pass lettuce, chicken, and oranges at the table family style. Pour on salad dressing. Top with candied almonds. Good served with multigrain crackers. Yield: 4 servings

BEFORE SERVING

Reserve broth and 4 chicken breasts from Asian Chicken Salad for:
- Creamy Chicken Alfredo
- Rainy Day Chicken-Rice Soup

Creamy Chicken Alfredo

¼ cup butter or margarine
¼ cup flour
1 cup chicken broth reserved from Asian Chicken Salad
OR 1 cup water and 1 teaspoon chicken soup base
1 cup heavy cream
2 tablespoons white wine
½ cup grated Parmesan cheese
1 (8-oz.) package fettuccine
2 reserved chicken breasts from Asian Chicken Salad (see page 13)

Melt butter or margarine over medium heat in a 3-quart saucepan. Add flour, stirring with a wooden spoon. Whisk in chicken broth and cream. Cook, stirring frequently, until thickened and bubbly (about 10 minutes). Add wine and cheese to sauce. Turn heat to very low. Cut chicken lengthwise into ½-inch strips; then cut crosswise to dice. Add chicken to sauce; keep warm while cooking pasta.

Cook fettuccine in a large pot of boiling water according to package directions. Drain pasta in a colander. Add pasta to chicken and sauce; serve as soon as possible. Pour into a large serving bowl or 2-quart casserole dish. Good served with spinach salad and Italian garlic bread. Yield: 4 servings

Low-fat variation: Replace cream with milk.

Rainy Day Chicken-Rice Soup

1 small onion
2 carrots
2 ribs celery
2 tablespoons oil
¼ teaspoon dried thyme
1 cup white or brown rice
Reserved broth from Asian Chicken Salad plus additional chicken broth to equal 6 cups
2 tablespoons corn starch
¼ cup water
2 reserved chicken breasts from Asian Chicken Salad (see page 13)
Salt and pepper to taste
1 tablespoon chopped fresh parsley
OR 1 teaspoon dried parsley

Using a chef's knife, cut onion in half on a cutting board. Peel off outer skin; cut out the root end. Place onion flat side down. Score; then cut to chop. Pare, rinse, and trim ends of carrots; cut in half crosswise. To prevent carrot from rolling, cut a flat edge, lengthwise. Cut lengthwise into slices. Then cut slices lengthwise into sticks; cut crosswise to dice. Rinse and trim ends and leaves of celery; cut in half crosswise. Cut lengthwise into sticks, then crosswise to dice.

Heat oil in a large (4-quart) pot on medium. Add onion, carrot, and celery and sauté for 5 minutes, stirring occasionally, until translucent. Add thyme, rice, and chicken broth. Bring to a boil over high heat. Turn down heat to low, cover, and simmer 20 minutes for white rice or 40 minutes for brown rice. Turn up heat to medium. Dissolve corn starch in ¼ cup water. Stir into soup to thicken. Cut chicken lengthwise into ½-inch strips; then cut crosswise to dice. Add chicken and simmer 2 additional minutes. Taste broth. Add salt and pepper, if needed.

For fresh parsley, place a small bunch in a colander and rinse under cold water. Rub the parsley with your fingers to remove dirt. Shake off excess water. Pat dry with a paper towel. Hold the parsley in a bunch and cut the leaves from the stems. Discard stems. Place leaves in a bowl and snip with kitchen shears or use a knife to chop on a cutting board. Add parsley just before serving. Good served with multigrain crackers and peanut or almond butter. Yield: 4 servings

Three-Day Plan

Day 1: Chicken Caesar Sandwiches ⟶ **Day 2:** Italian Chicken Spaghetti ⟶ **Day 3:** Chicken Ranch Wraps

Chicken Caesar Sandwiches

⅔ cup flour
2 eggs
1 teaspoon oil
1 cup grated Parmesan cheese
1 cup breadcrumbs
6 boneless, skinless chicken breasts
Salt and pepper
4 tablespoons butter or margarine, divided
4 tablespoons oil, divided
4 whole-wheat hamburger buns
2 tablespoons mayonnaise
1 tablespoon bottled Caesar salad dressing
4 green-leaf lettuce leaves

Pour flour on a sheet of waxed paper or a dinner plate. Beat eggs with 1 teaspoon oil in a medium-sized bowl. Mix Parmesan cheese and breadcrumbs in a pie plate. Place an extra sheet of waxed paper or plate nearby. Sprinkle chicken breasts with salt and pepper. Assembly-line style, dip each chicken breast first in flour (pat to remove extra flour), then in egg mixture, then in bread crumbs. Place breaded chicken breasts on waxed paper or plate to rest 10 minutes.

Heat 2 tablespoons butter or margarine and 2 tablespoons oil in a large skillet over medium-low heat. Use two skillets or cook in shifts. Do not crowd the pan. Sauté chicken breasts 7 - 8 minutes on each side (depending on the thickness) until brown and cooked through. Add more butter or margarine when needed. To serve, toast hamburger buns. Mix mayonnaise and Caesar dressing; spread on buns. Rinse lettuce and dry in a salad spinner (or pat dry with towels). Cut 2 chicken breasts in half and place on buns. Reserve remaining 4 chicken breasts for the next two meals. Top with lettuce. Good served with baked French fries and fresh tomato slices. Yield: 4 sandwiches

> ## BEFORE SERVING
> Reserve 4 chicken breasts from Chicken Caesar Sandwiches for:
> - Italian Chicken Spaghetti
> - Chicken Ranch Wraps

Italian Chicken Spaghetti

2 reserved chicken breasts from Chicken Caesar Sandwiches (see previous page)
1 (8-oz.) can tomato sauce
1 cup grated mozzarella cheese
¼ cup grated Parmesan cheese
1 (12-oz.) package angel hair pasta
2 tablespoons butter or margarine
1 tablespoon chopped fresh parsley
OR 1 teaspoon dried parsley

Cut chicken breasts crosswise into ½-inch slices. (Some breading might fall off.) Place chicken and breading in an 8x8 glass pan. Pour on tomato sauce. Top with mozzarella and Parmesan cheeses. Heat in a 325 degree F. oven for about 15 minutes or until chicken is warm and cheese is melted.

For fresh parsley, place a small bunch in a colander and rinse under cold water. Rub the parsley with your fingers to remove dirt. Shake off excess water. Pat dry with a paper towel. Hold the stems in a bunch and cut off the leaves. Discard stems. Place leaves in a bowl and snip with kitchen shears or use a knife to chop on a cutting board. Set aside.

Cook pasta according to package directions. Drain in a colander and rinse with cold water to stop the pasta from cooking. Return to pot over low heat. Add butter or margarine and parsley and stir until butter is melted. Plate pasta. Place chicken and sauce on top of pasta. Good served with creamed spinach and Italian garlic bread. Yield: 4 servings

Chicken Ranch Wraps

4 slices bacon
4 (burrito-size) flour tortillas
4 leaves green-leaf lettuce
2 reserved chicken breasts from Chicken Caesar Sandwiches (see page 18)
1 cup grated Cheddar cheese
Bottled Ranch dressing

Place bacon in a large skillet or on a griddle and fry over medium-low heat until crisp, turning occasionally. Drain on paper towels. Meanwhile, prepare the other ingredients.

Place each tortilla on a separate plate. Rinse lettuce and place in a salad spinner, rotating to dry (or pat dry with towels). Place one lettuce leaf on each tortilla. Thinly slice chicken breasts crosswise. (Some breading might come off.) Distribute chicken and breading on lettuce. Top with bacon and ¼ cup cheese. Pour on a tablespoon or two of Ranch dressing. Fold in lower edge of tortilla to keep filling in; then roll up tortilla from left to right. Good served with potato salad and coleslaw. Yield: 4 wraps

Three-Day Plan

Day 1: Spicy Chicken Picante ⟶ **Day 2:** Chicken & Barley Chili ⟶ **Day 3:** Cheesy Chicken Enchiladas

Spicy Chicken Picante

6 boneless, skinless chicken breasts
1 ½ cups bottled chunky picante sauce or salsa
3 tablespoons packed brown sugar
2 teaspoons prepared mustard
1 cup brown or white rice

Preheat oven to 400 degrees F. Place chicken breasts in a 3-quart casserole dish. Mix picante sauce or salsa, brown sugar, and mustard in a bowl. Pour over chicken. Bake 20 minutes covered; uncover and bake an additional 20 minutes until cooked through and bubbly.

Meanwhile, cook rice according to package directions. To retain juices, let chicken breasts rest for 10 minutes. Keep sauce warm in oven. Cut 3 chicken breasts into ¼-inch slices and mix with sauce. Reserve the remaining 3 chicken breasts for the next two meals. Serve chicken and spicy sauce over rice. Good served with sliced avocados. Yield: 4 servings

BEFORE SERVING

Reserve 3 chicken breasts from Spicy Chicken Picante for:
- Chicken & Barley Chili
- Cheesy Chicken Enchiladas

AFTER SERVING

Reserve any leftover sauce from Spicy Chicken Picante for:
- Chicken & Barley Chili

Chicken & Barley Chili

1 (14.5-oz.) can diced tomatoes
1 (16-oz.) can tomato sauce
Reserved sauce from Chicken Picante (see previous page)
1 (14.5-oz.) carton chicken broth
OR 1 ¾ cups water and 2 teaspoons chicken soup base
1 cup medium barley
4 cups water
1 tablespoon chili powder
1 teaspoon cumin
1 (15-oz.) can black beans
1 (15-oz.) can corn
1 reserved chicken breast from Baked Chicken Picante (see previous page)
1 cup grated Cheddar cheese
½ cup sour cream

Combine tomatoes, tomato sauce, sauce from Chicken Picante, chicken broth or water and soup base, barley, 4 cups water, chili powder, and cumin in a large 6 - 8 quart pot. Bring to a boil over high heat. Reduce heat to low, cover, and simmer 40 minutes, stirring occasionally.

Pour black beans into a colander or strainer; drain and rinse. Add black beans and corn (undrained) to pot. Cut chicken lengthwise into ½-inch strips; then cut crosswise to dice. Add chicken to pot; stir. Bring to a boil over high heat. Reduce heat to low, cover, and simmer 5 minutes. Ladle into soup bowls. Pass the cheese and sour cream at the table. Sprinkle chili with cheese and spoon on a dollop of sour cream. Good served with cornbread. Yield: 8 servings

Cheesy Chicken Enchiladas

8 flour tortillas
2 (10-oz.) cans enchilada sauce
2 reserved chicken breasts from Baked Chicken Picante (see page 21)
2 cups Colby-Jack cheese

Preheat oven to 350 degrees F. Grease a 9x13x2-inch pan. Pour about ⅓ of one can of enchilada sauce onto the bottom of the pan. Shred chicken by pulling it apart with 2 forks, or cut chicken lengthwise and crosswise to dice. In a medium-sized bowl, mix a few spoonfuls of the enchilada sauce with the chicken.

Place a tortilla on a plate. Spoon approximately one eighth of the chicken mixture onto the tortilla. Add 3 tablespoons cheese. Roll up tortilla jelly-roll style and place in prepared pan. Repeat with remaining tortillas, chicken mixture, and cheese, reserving the remaining cheese for the top. Pour the rest of the enchilada sauce on top of the tortillas, covering them completely. Cover the pan with foil and bake for 20 minutes or until warm. Remove foil and sprinkle with cheese. Place back in oven for 2 minutes or until cheese melts. Good served with Spanish rice and tortilla chips and salsa. Yield: 8 enchiladas

Three-Day Plan

Day 1: Grilled Honey-Lime Chicken ⟶ **Day 2:** Chicken Fajitas ⟶ **Day 3:** Chicken and Walnut Stir-Fry

Grilled Honey-Lime Chicken

8 boneless, skinless chicken breasts
2 limes
2 tablespoons butter or margarine
4 tablespoons honey
4 lettuce leaves
1 tomato
4 sandwich rolls
2 tablespoons mayonnaise

Position rack 6 inches above coals or gas fame. Cut limes in half and squeeze lime juice into a bowl. Stick a fork in the lime half and rub fork back and forth to squeeze as much juice as possible; repeat with other halves. Use a spoon to dip out and discard seeds. Melt butter or margarine in a small saucepan or in the microwave. Add to lime juice along with honey and stir.

Place chicken breasts on grill. Cook 8 minutes on each side, or until cooked through. Check with a meat thermometer, which should register 160 - 170 degrees F. To prevent the chicken from burning, wait to brush with lime mixture until just before removing from the grill.

Meanwhile, rinse and dry lettuce leaves. Rinse tomato. Cut out core and trim end; slice. Toast sandwich rolls and spread with mayonnaise. Place 4 chicken breasts on buns. Top with lettuce leaf and tomato slice. Reserve 4 chicken breasts for the following recipes. Good served with grilled corn on the cob and skewered grilled vegetables: onions, mushrooms, zucchini, and cherry tomatoes. Yield: 4 servings

BEFORE SERVING
Reserve 4 chicken breasts from Grilled Honey-Lime Chicken for:
- Chicken Fajitas
- Chicken and Walnut Stir-Fry

Chicken Fajitas

1 onion
1 green bell pepper
2 tablespoons oil
2 reserved chicken breasts from Grilled Honey-Lime Chicken (see previous page)
½ teaspoon chili powder
¼ teaspoon cumin
¼ teaspoon salt
1 lime
8 (soft taco-size) flour tortillas

Using a chef's knife, cut onion in half on a cutting board. Peel off outer skin; cut out the root end. Cut onion into thin slices. Rinse and cut green pepper in half. Pull out and discard seeds. Slice into strips. Heat oil in large skillet over medium heat. Add onion and pepper. Sauté about 5 minutes or until crisp-tender.

Add chicken and sauté for a minute or two, until heated. Add chili powder, cumin, and salt. Reduce heat to low. Cut lime in half and squeeze lime juice into a glass. Stick a fork in the lime half and rub fork back and forth to squeeze as much juice as possible. Use a spoon to dip out and discard seeds. Add juice to pan.

Heat tortillas in conventional oven or microwave oven according to package directions. Divide chicken and vegetables between tortillas. Roll up and serve. Good served with tortilla chips and a mixed green salad. Yield: 8 fajitas

Chicken and Walnut Stir-fry

1 medium green bell pepper
1 onion
1 cup fresh green beans
2 ribs celery
2 carrots
2 reserved chicken breasts from Grilled Honey-Lime Chicken (see page 24)
2 teaspoons cornstarch
2 tablespoons soy sauce
¾ cup chicken broth
OR ¾ cup water and ¾ teaspoon chicken soup base
1½ teaspoons vinegar
1 ½ teaspoons sugar
Dash hot pepper sauce
3 tablespoons oil
2 tablespoons water
⅔ cup walnut pieces
½ teaspoon ground ginger

Rinse and cut green pepper in half. Pull out and discard seeds. Slice into strips. Cut onion in half. Peel off outer skin; cut out the root end. Cut onion into thin slices. Rinse green beans; trim ends and snap in half, pulling off strings. Rinse and trim ends and leaves off of celery; slice diagonally into ¼-inch pieces. Pare, rinse, and trim ends off of carrots; slice diagonally into ¼-inch pieces. Cut chicken breast crosswise into ¼-inch strips. Measure cornstarch, soy sauce, broth or water and soup base, vinegar, sugar, and pepper sauce into a bowl; stir with a fork, and set aside.

Heat oil over medium-high heat in a wok or large skillet. Add green pepper, onion, green beans, celery, and carrots. Fry for 3 minutes while stirring. Add water, cover, and cook 2 - 3 minutes. Add chicken, walnuts, and ginger while stirring. Cook 1 minute. Add soy sauce mixture while stirring. Cook until bubbly and thickened. Good served over rice. Yield: 4 servings

Three-Day Plan

Day 1: Lemon Chicken ⟶ **Day 2:** California Salad ⟶ **Day 3:** Nine-Mile-High Tostadas

Lemon Chicken

1 tablespoon chopped fresh parsley
OR 1 teaspoon dried parsley flakes
½ cup flour, approximately
1 cup breadcrumbs, approximately
¼ teaspoon oregano
¼ teaspoon marjoram
¼ teaspoon basil
¼ teaspoon rosemary
2 eggs
6 boneless, skinless chicken breasts
6 tablespoons oil, divided
2 lemons

For fresh parsley, place a small bunch in a colander and rinse under cold water. Rub the parsley with your fingers to remove dirt. Shake off excess water. Pat dry with a paper towel. Hold the parsley in a bunch and cut the leaves from the stems. Discard stems. Place leaves in a bowl and snip with kitchen shears or use a knife to chop on a cutting board. Set aside.

Pour flour on a sheet of waxed paper or a dinner plate. Pour breadcrumbs beside flour. Sprinkle breadcrumbs with oregano, marjoram, basil, rosemary, and parsley and mix with a fork. Beat eggs in a medium-sized bowl with 1 tablespoon cold water. Place an extra sheet of waxed paper or separate plate nearby. Assembly-line style, dip each chicken breast first in flour (pat to remove extra flour), then in egg mixture, then in breadcrumbs. Add more breadcrumbs if needed. Place breaded chicken breasts on waxed paper or plate to rest for about 10 minutes.

Heat 3 tablespoons oil in a large skillet over medium heat. Use two skillets or cook in shifts. Do not crowd the pan. Sauté chicken breasts 5 minutes on each side until brown. Add more oil if needed. Slice one lemon, remove seeds, and place slices on chicken breasts. Cut and squeeze second lemon into a small bowl. Stick a fork in the lemon half and rub fork back and forth to squeeze as much juice as possible. Remove seeds and pour lemon juice over chicken. Cover and cook on low heat for about 20 minutes. Reserve 2 chicken breasts for the next two meals. Serve chicken breasts with lemon slices on top. Good served with brown rice and honeyed carrots. Yield: 4 servings

BEFORE SERVING

Reserve 2 chicken breasts from Lemon Chicken for:
- California Salad
- Nine-Mile-High Tostadas

California Salad

6 eggs
½ teaspoon salt
1 tablespoon vinegar
6 strips bacon
1 head romaine lettuce
2 tomatoes
1 avocado
2 oz. bleu cheese
1 cooked Lemon Chicken breast (see previous page)
2 tablespoons fresh snipped chives
Bottled vinaigrette salad dressing
Salt and freshly ground black pepper, to taste

To hard boil eggs, fill a medium-sized saucepan half full of water. Add salt and vinegar and bring to a boil over high heat. Turn heat to medium, and carefully slide eggs into water using a large spoon. Simmer 18 minutes. Partially cover with saucepan lid and pour off hot water, keeping eggs in the pan. Run cold water over eggs and add ice cubes to cool eggs quickly. Once cool, use a slotted spoon to move eggs to a bowl. Reserve 2 eggs for the next meal. Crack and roll eggs; peel. Discard shell and rinse eggs. Cut into slices; then cut across slices to dice. Set aside.

Place bacon in a large skillet or on a griddle and fry over medium-low heat until crisp. Drain on a paper towel. Crumble when cool. Preheat oven to 325 degrees F. Heat chicken breast for about 10 minutes until warm and crispy. Cut chicken breast lengthwise and then crosswise to dice. (Some breading might fall off.) While hard boiled eggs and bacon are cooking, and chicken is heating, prepare the other ingredients.

Using a large serrated bread knife, slice romaine lettuce into approximately 1-inch widths on a cutting board. Place lettuce in a large bowl and cover with cold water. Use your hand to stir the lettuce so dirt falls to the bottom. Gather the lettuce, carrying it up out of the water and into a salad spinner, rotating to dry (or pat dry with towels).

Rinse, core, and trim ends of tomatoes. Cut into ¼-inch slices; then cut across slices to dice. For avocado, slice through peel and flesh lengthwise cutting all the way around the pit. Pull apart to expose layers of peel, flesh, and pit. To easily remove the pit, cut the half with the pit lengthwise a second time. To dice, cut the avocado flesh into slices while still in peel. Remove peel with your fingers. Then cut the flesh crosswise into cubes. Crumble bleu cheese. Rinse chives under cool running water. Snip with a kitchen shears.

To serve, place a bed of lettuce on 4 dinner plates. Then place diced food in rows on top of lettuce: hard-boiled eggs, bacon, chicken, tomatoes, avocado, and bleu cheese. Sprinkle with chives. Pass the vinaigrette, salt, and peppermill at the table. Good served with multigrain crackers. Yield: 4 servings

Nine-Mile-High Tostadas

1 head iceberg lettuce
OR 1 (8-oz.) bag shredded iceberg lettuce
1 cooked Lemon Chicken breast (see page 27)
1 (15-oz.) can refried beans
1 cup grated Monterey-Jack cheese
1 tomato
1 onion
2 hard-boiled eggs reserved from California Salad (see previous page)
1 (12-count) box tostada shells
1 (12-oz.) carton sour cream
Bottled salsa

It's best to wash head lettuce a few hours or the night before using to allow for drainage. To wash lettuce, cut out core or rap core on counter hard enough to break it loose. Discard core. Turn lettuce head upside down and run under cold water allowing the water to push apart leaves and flow into the lettuce head. Turn core side down and place in a colander to drain. Store in the refrigerator wrapped in a tea towel or paper towels and a container or plastic bag to continue draining. Shred by cutting in half and then cutting into ¼-inch strips.

Preheat oven to 325 degrees F. Heat chicken breast for about 10 minutes until warm and crispy. Cut chicken breast crosswise in approximately ¼-inch slices. (Some breading might fall off.) Heat refried beans in a saucepan for about 5 minutes on medium. Rinse, core, and slice tomato into wedges. Using a chef's knife, cut onion in half on a cutting board. Peel off outer skin; cut out the root end. Cut onion into thin slices. Crack and roll hard boiled eggs; peel. Discard shell and rinse eggs; cut into slices. Heat 4 or more tostado shells according to package directions.

Serve family style by passing food at the table. Start with a bed of shredded lettuce on each plate. Spread a spoonful of refried beans on tostada shell. Sprinkle on a spoonful cheese and a few slices of chicken. Then pile on lettuce, tomato, onion, egg, sour cream and salsa. Yield: 4 servings

My Family Favorite Chicken Breast Three-Day Plan

Day 1: _____ ↗ **Day 2:** _____

↗ **Day 3:** _____

Where to find these recipes: _____

_____

_____

(Cookbook title with page #, recipe box, website, etc.)

BEFORE SERVING

Reserve _____ for:

- ♦ _____

- ♦ _____

Chapter 2: Whole Chickens

Types of Chickens

Recipes in this chapter include whole chickens. There are 3 types of chickens: broiler-fryers, roasters, and stewing hens. Chickens are named after a common way to cook them, but you can use any cooking method for broiler-fryers. They are younger and often weigh less than roasters and stewing hens, so broiler-fryers cook more quickly. I especially like to buy roasters because they are meaty and easy to cook by simply placing in the oven for an hour or so. Stewing hens are older, have tougher meat, and need to be cooked using moist-heat, simmering on the stove for a few hours.

Defrost Whole Chickens Safely

If chicken is frozen, defrost completely before you begin cooking. The best way to defrost a whole chicken is in the refrigerator where it takes about 2 days. If you defrost a whole chicken on the counter, submerge it in a large bowl of cold water and check every hour. If the water is not cold, dump, and add cold water to the bowl. Often the cavity of the chicken, where the neck and giblets are stored, takes the longest to defrost. Once the chicken is defrosted, refrigerate until ready to cook. When defrosting chicken in the microwave, cook it right away.

Don't Rinse

The rules have changed about rinsing chicken. I was taught to rinse chicken in cold water before preparing and pat dry with paper towels. However, there is a new guideline to skip rinsing chicken and simply pat it dry with paper towels. The reason to skip the rinsing step is that the sink, counter, and utensils will become contaminated. While rinsing was thought to help rid the chicken of bacteria, the bacteria will cook out of the chicken if cooked properly until done. To reduce the spread of bacteria, you need to wash your hands thoroughly with soap and water after touching chicken.

Freeze with Broth

To freeze cooked chicken, remove chicken from bone and cut into 1/2-inch cubes. Place 1- or 2-cup portions of diced chicken in freezer containers and cover with chicken broth. Frozen chicken covered with broth will keep up to 6 months. Frozen chicken without broth will keep up to 4 months.

For more information about food safety, see the U.S. Department of Agriculture (USDA) link: http://www.fsis.usda.gov/Help/FAQs_Food_Safety/index.asp

Three-Day Plan

Day 1: Mom's Chicken Noodle Soup ⟶ **Day 2:** Old-Fashioned Chicken Salad ⟶ **Day 3:** Homemade Chicken Pot Pie

Mom's Chicken Noodle Soup

1 (4 - 5 pound) broiler-fryer chicken
1 onion
2 carrots
2 ribs celery
6 oz. fine egg noodles
Salt and pepper to taste
Chicken soup base
1 tablespoon chopped fresh parsley
OR 1 teaspoon dried parsley

Place chicken and giblets in large pot. Fill with water just to cover. Trim ends and remove skin from onion. Pare, rinse, and cut 1 carrot into large pieces. Rinse, trim and cut 1 rib celery into large pieces. Add onion, carrot, and celery to pot. Bring to a boil, turn down heat and simmer for 15 minutes/pound of chicken, or 60 to 75 minutes.

Remove chicken and vegetables from pot; let cool until able to handle. Discard cooked vegetables—they helped to flavor the broth. Remove chicken from bone and cut into bite-sized pieces. You should have about 4 cups chicken; refrigerate. Discard bones. Pare, rinse, and trim ends of remaining carrot; cut in half crosswise. To prevent carrot from rolling, cut a flat edge, lengthwise. Cut carrot lengthwise into slices. Then cut slices lengthwise into sticks; cut crosswise to dice. Rinse and trim ends and leaves of remaining rib of celery; cut in half crosswise. Cut lengthwise into sticks, then crosswise to dice.

Skim fat from broth using a ladle; discard fat. Add diced vegetables. Bring broth to a boil. Cover, turn down heat, and simmer for 15 minutes. Add noodles and simmer for 5 minutes uncovered or according to package directions. Add 1 cup of diced chicken; reserve the remaining chicken for the next two recipes. Taste broth. Add soup base, salt, and pepper to taste.

For fresh parsley, place a small bunch in a colander and rinse under cold water. Rub the parsley with your fingers to remove dirt. Shake off excess water. Pat dry with a paper towel. Hold the parsley in a bunch and cut the leaves from the stems. Discard stems. Place leaves in a bowl and snip with kitchen shears or use a knife to chop on a cutting board. Add parsley to soup. Good served with crackers, sliced Cheddar cheese, and apple slices. Yield: 4 servings

BEFORE SERVING

Reserve 3 cups diced chicken from Mom's Chicken Noodle Soup for:
- Old-Fashioned Chicken Salad
- Homemade Chicken Pot Pie

Old-Fashioned Chicken Salad

3 eggs
1 tablespoon cider vinegar
2 ribs celery
2 cups diced, cooked chicken from Mom's Chicken Noodle Soup (see previous page)
¼ teaspoon salt
Dash pepper
1 lemon
½ cup mayonnaise
2 small cantaloupes

First, hard boil eggs. Bring a medium-sized saucepan half full of water to a boil over high heat. Turn heat to medium, add vinegar, and carefully slide eggs into water using a large spoon. Simmer 18 minutes. Partially cover and pour off hot water, keeping eggs in the pan. Run cold water over eggs and add ice cubes to cool eggs quickly. Once cool, use slotted spoon to move eggs to a bowl. Crack and roll eggs; peel. Discard shell and rinse eggs. Dice and place in a large mixing bowl.

Rinse and trim ends and leaves of celery; cut in half crosswise. Cut lengthwise into sticks, then crosswise to dice. Add celery and chicken to bowl. Add salt and pepper. Cut and squeeze lemon into a separate, small bowl. Stick a fork in the lemon half and rub fork back and forth to squeeze as much juice as possible. Discard seeds and lemon rind. Add juice to bowl along with mayonnaise; stir.

Rinse cantaloupes; cut in half. Scoop out and discard seeds. Divide the chicken salad between the four cantaloupe halves. Good served with whole-grain rolls. Yield: 4 servings

Homemade Chicken Pot Pie

Dough for 2-crust pie:
2 cups flour
½ teaspoon salt
⅔ cup shortening, butter, or margarine
½ cup cold water, approximately

For filling:
2 tablespoons butter or margarine
2 tablespoons flour
1½ cups chicken broth
OR 1½ cups water and 1½ teaspoons chicken soup base
Salt and pepper to taste
1 cup frozen mixed vegetables
1 cup diced, cooked chicken from Mom's Chicken Noodle Soup (see page 34)

Easy variation: Buy prepared pie dough.

For pie dough, measure and mix flour and salt in a medium-sized bowl. Cut in shortening, butter, or margarine with a pastry blender or 2 knives until it resembles meal. Stir in ¼ cup water with a fork. Add additional water, 1 tablespoon at a time, just until dough is mixed and pulls away from the sides. Let dough rest 15 minutes in freezer or 1 hour in refrigerator.

Meanwhile, make filling. For gravy, melt butter or margarine in a saucepan over medium heat. Add flour, stirring until hot and bubbly. Remove from heat and whisk in chicken broth. Return to burner on medium heat, and stir constantly with a wooden spoon until thickened. Add salt and pepper to taste. Add vegetables and chicken.

Preheat oven to 425 degrees F. Divide pie dough in half. Roll out one portion of dough by rolling from the center outward into a 12-inch circle about ¼ inch thick. Place in a 9-inch pie plate (deep dish if you have one) for bottom crust. Pour filling into pastry-lined pie plate.

Roll out remaining dough into an 11-inch circle about ¼ inch thick for top crust. Fold top crust in half; then fold in half again to make a triangle with a curved edge. Use a butter knife to make 4 small slits, 2 on each fold, to allow steam to escape. Place triangle of dough on filling with the point in the center; unfold top crust, revealing slits. Fold any excess dough from the top crust under the edge of the bottom crust. Crimp edges with floured fingers. To crimp, pinch dough with thumb and pointer finger of left hand and press pointer finger from right hand into pinched dough to form a raised edge. Repeat all the way around the rim of the pie.

Cover edge of piecrust with pie shield or strips of aluminum foil. Bake at 425 degrees F. for 10 minutes; then turn heat down to 375 degrees F. for 30 - 40 minutes or until light brown, removing pie shield for the last 15 minutes of baking to brown crust. Good served with a mixed green salad. Filling is very hot, so use caution. Yield: 1 pie; 4 - 6 servings

Three-Day Plan

Day 1: Spanish-Style Chicken ⟶ **Day 2:** Cheesy Chicken Quesadillas ⟶ **Day 3:** Brunswick Stew

Spanish-Style Chicken

1 onion
1 rib celery
1 (4 - 5 pound) broiler-fryer chicken
Salt and pepper
1 clove garlic
1 (16-oz.) can chopped tomatoes
2 teaspoons beef soup base
1 teaspoon paprika
1 (12-oz.) package fully cooked, cocktail-size, smoked sausages
3 tablespoons flour

Using a chef's knife, cut onion in half on a cutting board. Peel off outer skin and cut out the root end. Score and chop onion. Rinse, trim ends, and cut celery crosswise into ½-inch pieces. Place onion and celery in a slow cooker. Sprinkle chicken with salt and pepper, and place in slow cooker. (If chicken doesn't fit in slow cooker, either cut it up or use a large pot and cook on the stove over lowest heat and cut the cooking time in half.) Press the flat side of a chef's knife on garlic clove to break skin. Peel off skin. Trim off root end. Score; then cut to mince. Add garlic, tomatoes with juice, soup base, and paprika to slow cooker. Cover and cook on high setting for 2 hours. Add sausages, cover, and cook an additional hour.

Use a slotted spoon to remove sausages and vegetables to a casserole dish; cover and keep warm in a 250 degree F. oven. Place chicken to a cutting board. Let rest 10 minutes. First cut off the thighs and legs. Then cut the leg from the thigh. Cut off the wings; then cut down the breast bone as you pull off the breast meat from the bone. Reserve 1 chicken breast, 1 thigh, and 1 wing for the next 2 recipes. Keep the rest of the chicken warm with the sausage and vegetables. Use a ladle to skim the fat from the broth. Using a fork or wire whisk, blend flour into ⅓ cup cold water. Whisk into broth. Cover and cook until thick and bubbly, about 15 minutes. Serve gravy over chicken, sausages, and vegetables. Good served over rice. Reserve any leftover vegetables and sauce for Brunswick Stew. Yield: 4 servings

BEFORE SERVING

Reserve 1 chicken breast, 1 chicken thigh, and 1 wing from Spanish-Style Chicken for:
- Cheesy Chicken Quesadillas
- Brunswick Stew

AFTER SERVING

Reserve any leftover vegetables and sauce from Spanish-Style Chicken for:
- Brunswick Stew

Cheesy Chicken Quesadillas

1 tablespoon oil
Reserved chicken breast from Spanish-Style Chicken (see previous page)
2 tablespoons butter or margarine
1 package (8-count) medium-size flour tortillas
Bottled picante sauce
1 cup grated Cheddar cheese

Remove chicken breast from bone. Discard bone and finely dice chicken. Heat oil in a large, nonstick skillet over medium heat. Spread a tortilla with butter or margarine. Place tortilla in skillet buttered side down.

Spoon and spread about a fourth of the chicken on the tortilla. Add a spoonful of picante sauce and sprinkle with ¼ cup cheese. Spread a second tortilla with butter or margarine. Top chicken and cheese, placing this tortilla buttered side up. Turn after a few minutes when bottom tortilla is lightly browned. Fry lightly until second side is lightly browned and cheese is melted.

Keep warm on a cookie sheet in a 200 degree F. oven. Repeat with remaining ingredients. Cut into wedges before serving. Good served with roasted potatoes and a mixed green salad. Yield: 4 servings

Brunswick Stew

Reserved vegetables and sauce from Spanish-Style Chicken (see page 38)
2 red potatoes
3 cups broth
OR 3 cups water and 3 teaspoons soup base
2 tablespoons red or white wine
1 teaspoon Worcestershire sauce
1 (10-oz) package frozen corn
1 (10-oz) package frozen baby lima beans
Reserved thigh and wing from Spanish-Style Chicken (See page 38)

Place reserved vegetables and sauce in a large (4-quart) pot. Pare and rinse potatoes. Cut into ½-inch slices, cut into sticks, and dice into cubes. Add to pot along with broth or water and soup base, wine, and Worcestershire sauce.

Bring to a boil over high heat. Add corn and lima beans and return to boil. Turn down to low, cover, and simmer 30 minutes or until lima beans are soft. Meanwhile, remove chicken thigh and wing from bones. Discard bones and cut chicken into bite-sized pieces. Add chicken to pot. Simmer 5 minutes more. Serve in bowls. Good served with buttery biscuits. Yield: 4 servings

Three-Day Plan

Day 1: Herb-Roasted Chicken ⟶ **Day 2:** Chicken Salad with Sugar-Glazed Pecans ⟶ **Day 3:** Jambalaya

Herb-Roasted Chicken

1 (5 - 7 pound) roasting hen
OR 2 (3 - 4 pound) broiler-fryer chickens
Salt
¼ teaspoon rosemary
¼ teaspoon thyme
¼ teaspoon dried parsley

Preheat oven to 375 degrees F. Place chicken, breast side up, in a shallow roasting pan and pat dry with paper towels. Remove the heart, gizzard, liver, and neck from the inner cavity. Leave them in the roasting pan to give the broth a good flavor.

Using a salt shaker, lightly shake salt to distribute evenly inside the chicken cavity and out. Crush rosemary, thyme, and parsley with your fingers as you sprinkle it over the breast and legs. Pull off the two lumps of fat in the inner cavity and place them on top of the breast to baste the chicken to keep it moist. Bake, uncovered, at 375 degrees F. for about 1 ¼ to 2 ¼ hours (20 minutes per pound) or until breast is brown and juices run clear when leg-thigh joint is pierced and meat thermometer registers 170.

Let chicken rest for 10 minutes before carving. First cut off the thighs and legs and place on serving platter. Then cut the leg from the thigh. Cut off the wings; then cut down the breast bone as you pull off the breast meat from the bone. Before serving, reserve 1 chicken breast and 1 thigh if you've cooked a 5 - 7 pound roasting chicken, or reserve 2 chicken breasts and 2 chicken thighs if you've roasted two 3 - 4 pound chickens for the next two recipes. Good served with roasted vegetable medley. Yield: 4 servings

BEFORE SERVING

Reserve 1 - 2 chicken breasts and 1 - 2 thighs from Herb-Roasted Chicken for:
- Chicken Salad with Sugar-Glazed Pecans
- Jambalaya

Chicken Salad with Sugar-Glazed Pecans

¼ cup sugar
1 cup pecan pieces
1 head green leaf or Romaine lettuce
1 - 2 reserved chicken breast(s) from Herb-Roasted Chicken (see previous page)
1 cup grated Cheddar or crumbled blue cheese
1 cup dried cranberries
Bottled balsamic-vinaigrette dressing

Place a sheet of waxed paper on a cookie sheet; set aside. For candied pecan topping, pour ¼ cup sugar into a small skillet. Melt sugar over low heat, which takes 5 - 10 minutes. Watch closely; sugar can burn. As soon as the sugar dissolves into a light brown liquid quickly add pecans and carefully stir with a metal spatula. Note: melted sugar is very hot! Spread candied pecans onto waxed paper-lined cookie sheet to cool. Once cool, crumble and place in a serving bowl.

Either tear lettuce or use a large serrated knife to slice green leaf or Romaine lettuce into approximately 1-inch widths on a cutting board. Place lettuce in a large bowl and cover with cold water. Use your hand to stir the lettuce so dirt can fall to the bottom. Gather the lettuce, carrying it up out of the water and into a salad spinner, rotating to dry (or pat dry with towels). Place in a large salad bowl.

Cut chicken breast(s) lengthwise, then crosswise to dice. Add to lettuce along with cheese and cranberries. Pour on salad dressing and toss. Pass candied pecans at table. Good served with crescent rolls. Yield: 4 servings

Jambalaya

1 onion
1 green pepper
1 rib celery
1 tablespoon oil
Reserved chicken thigh(s) from Herb-Roasted Chicken (see page 41)
1 (16-oz.) package smoked sausage such as Polska Kielbasa
1 (14 ½-oz.) can diced tomatoes
½ teaspoon salt
1 teaspoon hot pepper sauce
1 tablespoon chopped fresh parsley
OR 1 teaspoon dried parsley

Using a chef's knife, cut onion in half on a cutting board. Peel off outer skin; cut out the root end. Cut onion into thin slices. Rinse and cut green pepper in half. Pull out and discard seeds. Slice into strips. Rinse and trim ends of celery; cut in half. Slice celery into strips and then cut crosswise to dice.

Heat oil in large skillet on medium. Add onion, pepper, and celery. Sauté about 5 minutes or until crisp-tender. Meanwhile, cut sausage in half lengthwise and crosswise into ½-inch pieces. Add to skillet and cook for about 3 minutes until lightly browned. Remove chicken breast from bone; dice. Add chicken, tomatoes with juice, salt, and pepper sauce to skillet. Bring to a boil; then turn down heat to low, cover and simmer for about 10 minutes.

For fresh parsley, place a small bunch in a colander and rinse under cold water. Rub the parsley with your fingers to remove dirt. Shake off excess water. Pat dry with a paper towel. Hold the parsley in a bunch and cut the leaves from the stems. Discard stems. Place leaves in a bowl and snip with kitchen shears or use a knife to chop on a cutting board. Sprinkle with parsley. Good served over brown rice. Yield: 4 servings

Three-Day Plan

Day 1: Chicken 'n Dumplings ⟶ **Day 2:** Everybody's Favorite Chicken Pasta Salad ⟶ **Day 3:** BBQ Chicken Sandwiches

Chicken 'n Dumplings

1 (5-pound) stewing hen
OR 1 (5-pound) roasting hen
1 onion
2 carrots
2 ribs celery
3 tablespoons flour
salt and pepper to taste
chicken soup base

Easy variation: Replace dumpling dough with 2 cups biscuit mix. Follow box directions, stirring in milk to make biscuit dough, and dropping tablespoonsful of biscuit dough onto hot gravy.

For dumplings:
1½ cups flour
2 teaspoons baking powder
½ teaspoon salt
3 tablespoons shortening or margarine
¾ cup milk

Remove giblets from cavity and place chicken in a large pot. Fill with water to cover. Trim ends and remove skin from onion; add to pot. Pare, rinse, trim ends, and cut 1 carrot into large pieces; add to pot. Rinse, trim ends, and cut 1 rib celery into large pieces; add to pot. Bring to a boil, turn down heat and simmer 30 minutes/pound for stewing hen, 2½ hours, OR 20 minutes/pound for roasting hen, 1¾ hours.

Remove chicken and vegetables from pot; let cool until able to handle. Discard cooked vegetables—they helped to flavor the broth. Remove chicken from bone and cut into bite-sized pieces. Discard bones. Divide the chicken in thirds. Use a third of the chicken (about 1½ cups) for this recipe and reserve the remaining chicken for the next two recipes. Refrigerate chicken while you make the gravy and dumplings.

Using a ladle, skim the fat from the top of the broth. Measure 3 tablespoons of chicken fat into a large skillet; discard the remaining fat. Heat the chicken fat in skillet on medium. Add 3 tablespoons flour, stirring until bubbly. Remove from heat and whisk in 3 cups chicken broth. (Reserve the remaining broth for another recipe.) Heat to boiling over medium-high heat; then turn down to low. Taste; add salt and pepper or chicken soup base if needed.

For dumplings, measure and mix flour, baking powder and salt in a medium-sized bowl. Cut in shortening or margarine with a pastry blender or 2 knives. Stir in milk with a fork. Drop tablespoonsful of dough onto bubbling gravy. Cook gently for 10 minutes; then cover and cook on the lowest heat for an additional 20 minutes. Add 1 ½ cups diced chicken in between dumplings; heat for a few minutes. Serve chicken and dumplings with plenty of gravy. Good served with mashed potatoes and fresh green beans. Yield: 4 servings

BEFORE SERVING

Reserve 3 cups diced chicken from Chicken 'n Dumplings for:
- Everybody's Favorite Chicken Pasta Salad
- BBQ Chicken Sandwiches

Everybody's Favorite Chicken Pasta Salad

1 (8-oz) package large shell pasta
1 stalk fresh broccoli
1 carrot
1 cup frozen peas
1 green pepper
1 small red onion
1 (5-oz.) jar olives
1 (5-oz.) package sliced pepperoni
1 cup diced mozzarella cheese
½ cup Parmesan cheese
1 ½ cups diced, cooked chicken reserved from Chicken 'n Dumplings (see page 45)
1 (8-oz.) bottle Italian dressing

Cook shell pasta according to package directions. Drain in colander and rinse with cold running water. Pour into big mixing bowl. Rinse and trim broccoli. Cut tops (florets) into bite-sized pieces on a cutting board. Pare, rinse, trim ends off carrot. Cut in half crosswise. Trim an edge, lengthwise, to keep carrot from rolling. Cut into ¼-inch rounds. Fill a small saucepan with about an inch of water; bring to a boil over high heat. Add broccoli, carrots, and peas. Return to boil, cover, turn down heat to medium-low and simmer for 5 minutes. Drain and cool.

Rinse and cut green pepper in half. Pull out and discard seeds. Cut into strips; then cut across strips to dice. Cut onion in half lengthwise. Peel off outer skin; cut out the root end. Place onion flat side down. Score onion. Cut across the onion to dice.

Drain olives; slice. Cut pepperoni slices in half. Add all to pasta: broccoli, carrots, peas, green pepper, onion, olives, pepperoni, mozzarella cheese, Parmesan cheese, chicken, and dressing. After mixing, refrigerate until ready to serve. Good made the day before so the flavors can blend. Good served with Italian garlic bread. Yield: 4 - 6 servings

BBQ Chicken Sandwiches

1 ½ cups diced, cooked chicken reserved from Chicken 'n Dumplings (see page 45)
About 1 cup bottled BBQ sauce
4 multigrain sandwich rolls

Place chicken in a small saucepan and pour on BBQ sauce; stir. Heat over medium-low heat until warm and bubbly, stirring occasionally. Toast buns. Spoon chicken and sauce onto buns. Good served with baked sweet potato fries and coleslaw. Yield: 4 servings

My Family Favorite Whole Chicken Three-Day Plan

Day 1: _____ ⤳ **Day 2:** _____

⤳ **Day 3:** _____

Where to find these recipes: _____

_____

_____

(*Cookbook title with page #, recipe box, website, etc.*)

BEFORE SERVING

Reserve _____ for:

- _____
- _____

Delicious Dinners with Turkey

Chapter 3: Whole Turkeys

Purchasing Turkey

When planning a meal featuring turkey, allow 1 pound per person. A 20-pound turkey will feed 20 people. Plan for leftover turkey, too. A 20-pound turkey will feed 12 people with leftovers for 8. You can freeze leftover Thanksgiving turkey to enjoy in the spring. Turkey freezes for up to 6 months when frozen in broth.

Defrosting Turkey

If turkey is frozen, defrost completely before you begin cooking. Turkeys are heavier than chickens and take longer to thaw. The best way to defrost turkey is in the refrigerator, which can take nearly a week, depending on the size. When thawing a turkey in the refrigerator, allow 24 hours for every 4 - 5 pounds of turkey. For example, 3 days for a 12-pound turkey and 6 days for a 24-pound turkey. If you defrost turkey on the counter, submerge it in a large bowl or roasting pan of cold water and check every hour. If the water is not cold, dump, and add cold water to the bowl. It will take about 30 minutes to defrost each pound of turkey, 6 hours for a 12-pound turkey and 12 hours for a 24-pound turkey.

For more on information about turkey, see the United States Department of Agriculture (USDA) link:
http://www.fsis.usda.gov/factsheets/lets_talk_turkey/index.asp

Three-Day Plan

Day 1: Basic Roast Turkey ⟶ **Day 2:** Hot Turkey Sandwiches with Gravy ⟶ **Day 3:** Homemade Turkey Soup with Pasta

Basic Roast Turkey

12 to 24 pound turkey
1 tablespoon butter or margarine
Salt
1 onion
1 rib celery
1 carrot

Preheat oven to 325 degrees F. Remove the giblets (heart, gizzard, liver) and neck from the inner cavity. Place breast side up in a large roasting pan on a wire rack. Pat dry with a paper towel. Rub skin all over with butter or margarine. Sprinkle with salt inside and out. Place giblets and neck in pan with turkey or cook separately for giblet gravy.

Trim and rinse celery; cut into large pieces. Pare, rinse, and trim carrots; cut crosswise into large pieces. Trim ends of onion, keeping onion whole. Peel off outer skin. Add onion, carrot, and celery to roaster pan to flavor the broth. Bake approximately 20 minutes per pound. For example, 4 hours for a 12-pound turkey and 8 hours for a 24-pound turkey. Test by piercing with a fork between leg and thigh to see if juices run clear. A meat thermometer should register 185 degrees F.

Let turkey set for 20 minutes before carving. Using a carving knife, first cut off the thighs, including the legs. Then cut the leg from the thigh. Cut off the wings. To remove breast from bone, cut down the breastbone while pulling to separate breast from turkey. Then cut crosswise into slices. Arrange turkey on serving platter. Use the drippings for gravy after removing the vegetables, giblets, and neck, and skimming the fat from the broth. Before serving, reserve ½ of one of the turkey breasts, 1 of the thighs, and the turkey frame (back and ribs) for the next two meals. For a traditional Thanksgiving meal, serve with: gravy, stuffing, cranberry sauce, candied sweet potatoes, and green bean casserole. Yield: 12 to 40 servings, depending on the size of the turkey

BEFORE SERVING

Reserve ½ turkey breast, 1 thigh, and the frame (back and ribs) from Basic Roast Turkey for:
- Hot Turkey Sandwiches with Gravy
- Homemade Turkey Soup with Pasta

AFTER SERVING

After reserving half of turkey breast and 1 thigh for the next 2 dinners, bone, dice, and place remaining turkey in 2-cup freezer containers. Pour turkey broth or chicken broth to cover diced turkey. Use in the following recipes. (Use both the turkey and broth in the recipes.) Note: Frozen turkey covered in broth will keep up to 6 months. Frozen turkey without broth will keep up to 4 months.
- Turkey Tetrazzini
- Turkey 'n Corn Chili
- Turkey à La King
- Deep-Dish Turkey with Almonds
- Turkey Salad Wraps
- Creamy Turkey Noodle Casserole

Hot Turkey Sandwiches with Gravy

4 tablespoons butter or margarine
6 tablespoons flour
3 cups turkey or chicken broth
OR 3 cups water and 1 tablespoon chicken soup base
Salt and pepper to taste
Reserved half of turkey breast from Roast Turkey (see page 51)
4 slices bread

Melt butter or margarine in a medium (2-quart) saucepan. Add flour, stirring constantly, and cook until lightly browned. Whisk in turkey or chicken broth, or water and chicken soup base. Bring to a boil over medium heat, stirring frequently. Turn down heat to low. Add salt and pepper to taste. Thinly slice turkey and add to gravy. Toast bread and cut into fourths diagonally. Place 2-4 toast points on each plate. Ladle turkey and gravy over toast points. Good served with garlic mashed potatoes and roasted asparagus. Yield: 4 servings

Homemade Turkey Soup with Pasta

Reserved turkey frame (back and ribs) from Basic Roast Turkey (see page 51)
2 ribs celery
2 carrots
1 cup frozen corn
1 cup frozen green beans
1 cup small shell pasta, uncooked
Reserved turkey thigh from Basic Roast Turkey (see page 51)
2 teaspoons chicken soup base
Salt and pepper to taste

Place turkey frame in a large (8-quart) pot and cover with cold water. Bring to a boil; turn down heat to low. Cover and simmer for an hour or two. Remove any additional turkey from frame and refrigerate. Discard frame.

Trim and rinse celery. Cut in half crosswise, then lengthwise in sticks. To dice, cut across sticks. Pare, rinse, and trim off ends of carrot. Cut in half lengthwise; then place flat side down so carrot won't roll. Cut in ¼-inch slices. Add to pot. Bring to a boil; then turn down heat to low. Cover and simmer 20 minutes.

Turn up heat and bring to a boil. Add corn, green beans, and pasta. Turn down heat to medium-low and simmer for 10 minutes uncovered. Cut meat off turkey thigh bone. Add meat to soup along with refrigerated turkey from frame. Add chicken soup base and taste. Add salt and pepper if needed. Good served with bread sticks and a mixed green salad. Yield: 4 servings

Weekly Plans

Use frozen turkey once/week in these recipes. Defrost in refrigerator the night before, or defrost in the microwave.

Week 1: Turkey Tetrazzini ⟶ **Week 2:** Turkey 'n Corn Chili ⟶ **Week 3:** Turkey à La King ⟶ **Week 4:** Deep-Dish Turkey with Almonds ⟶ **Week 5:** Turkey Salad Wraps ⟶ **Week 6:** Creamy Turkey Noodle Casserole

Turkey Tetrazzini

1 (7-oz.) package spaghetti
1 (8-oz.) package button mushrooms
3 tablespoons butter or margarine, divided
2 tablespoons oil, divided
¼ cup flour
½ teaspoon salt
1 cup chicken broth
OR 1 cup water and 1 teaspoon chicken soup base
1 cup whipping cream
2 cups diced turkey from Basic Roast Turkey (see page 51)
2 tablespoons sherry or dry white wine
½ cup grated Parmesan cheese

Cook spaghetti according to package directions; drain and set aside. Preheat oven to 350 degrees F. Place mushrooms in a bowl of cool water. Stir with hands; dirt will fall to the bottom of the bowl. To prevent mushrooms from absorbing water, do not let soak. Remove mushrooms from water and place on a cutting board. Slice about ¼ inch thick. Heat 1 tablespoon butter or margarine and 1 tablespoon oil in a large skillet over medium/medium-high heat. Sauté mushrooms, stirring frequently, for about 2-3 minutes, until just cooked. Remove from skillet and set aside.

Add the remaining 2 tablespoons of butter or margarine and tablespoon of oil to the skillet and heat on medium until butter is melted. Stir in flour, cooking until bubbly. Whisk in broth and cream. Cook over medium heat until thickened, stirring constantly. Add wine, turkey, and spaghetti. Drain and add mushrooms. Pour into an ungreased 2-quart casserole. Sprinkle with cheese. Bake uncovered 30 minutes or until hot and bubbly. Good served with stir-fried broccoli. Yield: 4 servings

Turkey 'n Corn Chili

1 tablespoon oil
2 cloves garlic
1 medium onion
1 (15-oz.) can great northern beans
1 (15-oz.) can corn
1 (7-oz.) can chopped mild green chilies
4 cups chicken broth
OR 4 cups water and 4 teaspoons chicken soup base
1 teaspoon ground cumin
¾ teaspoon oregano leaves
⅛ teaspoon cayenne pepper
2 cups diced turkey from Basic Roast Turkey (see page 51)
Salt to taste
Grated white Cheddar or Monterey Jack cheese
Bottled salsa
Sour cream

Heat oil in a large (4-quart) pot on medium. Using a chef's knife, cut onion in half lengthwise on a cutting board. Peel off outer skin; cut out the root end. Place onion flat side down. Score; then cut to dice. Press the flat side of a chef's knife on garlic clove to break skin. Peel off skin. Trim off root end. Score; then cut to mince. Sauté onion about 5 minutes; add garlic and sauté 2 additional minutes.

Drain and rinse beans and add to pot. Add corn with liquid, chilies, broth or water and soup base, cumin, oregano and cayenne pepper. Bring to a boil over high heat. Reduce heat to low, cover, and simmer 1 hour. Add turkey. Taste and add salt if needed. Serve in bowls; sprinkle with cheese and spoon on salsa and sour cream at the table. Good served with tortilla chips. Yield: 4 servings

Turkey à la King

2 ounces (about 4 medium) button mushrooms
1 green bell pepper
3 tablespoons butter or margarine, divided
2 tablespoons oil, divided
3 tablespoons flour
1 cup chicken broth
OR 1 cup water and 1 teaspoon chicken soup base
½ cup heavy cream
2 cups diced turkey from Basic Roast Turkey (see page 51)
1 tablespoon chopped fresh parsley
OR 1 teaspoon dried parsley
1 cup frozen green peas
2 egg yolks
3 tablespoons sherry or dry white wine
Salt and pepper to taste
4 slices bread

Place mushrooms in a bowl of cool water. Stir with hands; dirt will fall to the bottom of the bowl. To prevent mushrooms from absorbing water, do not soak. Remove mushrooms from water and place on a cutting board. Slice about ¼ inch thick. Set aside. Rinse and cut green pepper in half. Pull out and discard seeds. Slice pepper into ½-inch strips; then cut across strips to dice.

Place fresh parsley in a colander and rinse under cold water. Rub the parsley with your fingers to remove dirt. Shake off excess water. Pat dry with a paper towel. Hold the parsley in a bunch and cut the leaves from the stems. Discard stems. Place leaves in a bowl and snip with kitchen shears or use a knife to chop on a cutting board. Set aside.

Heat 1 tablespoon oil and 1 tablespoon butter or margarine in a large skillet over medium/medium-high heat. Sauté mushrooms, stirring frequently, for 2 - 3 minutes, until just cooked. Remove from skillet and set aside. Turn heat down to medium. Add 1 tablespoon oil and 2 tablespoons butter or margarine to skillet and sauté green pepper for 3 minutes. Add flour, stirring. Whisk in broth, stirring until thick and bubbly. Stir in cream. Add the turkey, parsley, and peas. Bring to a boil; then turn down heat to low. Simmer 5 minutes.

Beat egg yolks and sherry. Gradually beat a few tablespoons of hot chicken broth mixture into the egg yolk mixture to acclimate the egg yolks to the warmer temperature. Then whisk the egg yolk mixture into the skillet. To prevent curdling, do not allow to boil. Drain mushrooms and add to skillet. Season to taste with salt and pepper. Toast bread and cut into fourths diagonally. Place 4 triangles on each plate. Ladle turkey and sauce over toast. Good served with mashed potatoes. Yield: 4 servings

Deep-Dish Turkey with Almonds

¼ of an onion
4 ribs celery
3 cups diced turkey from Basic Roast Turkey (see page 51)
1 cup real mayonnaise
1 lemon
½ cup slivered almonds
½ teaspoon salt
Pinch pepper
½ cup grated sharp Cheddar cheese
¼ cup dry whole-wheat breadcrumbs
2 tablespoons butter or margarine

Preheat oven to 450 degrees F. Grease a 1½-quart casserole dish. Grate onion. Rinse and trim celery; cut in half. Cut lengthwise into strips; then cut across strips to dice. Cut and squeeze second lemon into a small bowl. Stick a fork in the lemon half and rub fork back and forth to squeeze as much juice as possible. Remove seeds. Place ingredients in prepared casserole dish: onion, celery, turkey, mayonnaise, lemon juice, almonds, salt, and pepper. Stir to combine. Sprinkle with cheese and breadcrumbs. Melt butter or margarine. Drizzle over breadcrumbs. Bake for 15 minutes. Good served over rice with honeyed carrots.
Yield: 4 servings

Turkey Salad Wraps

1/2 teaspoon salt
2 eggs
1 tablespoon vinegar
1 green bell pepper
2 ribs celery
2 cups diced turkey from Basic Roast Turkey (see page 51)
⅓ cup mayonnaise
4 wheat flour tortillas
4 lettuce leaves

To hard boil eggs, fill a small (1-quart) saucepan half full of water. Add salt and bring to a boil over high heat. Turn heat to medium, add vinegar, and carefully slide eggs into water using a large spoon. Simmer 18 minutes. To drain water from eggs, partially cover with lid, and pour hot water into kitchen sink, keeping eggs in the pan. Run cold water over eggs and add ice cubes to cool eggs quickly. Once cool, crack and roll eggs; peel eggs. Discard shell and rinse eggs. Dice and place in a mixing bowl.

Rinse and cut green pepper in half. Pull out and discard seeds. Slice into thin strips; then cut crosswise to dice. Rinse and trim ends and leaves of celery; cut in half crosswise. Cut lengthwise into thin sticks, then crosswise to dice. Drain turkey if it was frozen with broth. Add pepper and celery to mixing bowl, along with turkey. Add mayonnaise, stirring to combine. Rinse and spin lettuce dry in a salad spinner, or pat lettuce dry with towels. Place one lettuce leaf on each tortilla. Spoon turkey salad onto lettuce. Fold up bottom edge to keep filling in; then roll from left to right. Good served with vegetable soup. Yield: 4 servings

Creamy Turkey Noodle Casserole

1 (8-oz.) package noodles
2 tablespoons butter or margarine
2 tablespoons flour
1 ½ cup milk
¼ cup Parmesan cheese
2 cups diced turkey from Basic Roast Turkey (see page 51)
¼ cup breadcrumbs
1 tablespoon butter or margarine

Preheat oven to 350 degrees F. Grease a 2-quart casserole dish. Cook noodles according to package directions; drain. Melt butter or margarine in a large saucepan. Stir in flour. Add milk and stir constantly until boiling. Remove from heat and add cheese, turkey, and noodles. Pour into prepared casserole dish. Sprinkle with breadcrumbs and dot with butter or margarine. Bake for 20 to 30 minutes or until bubbling. Good served with braised cabbage. Yield: 4 servings

My Family Favorite Turkey Three-Day Plan

Day 1: _____ ⟶ **Day 2:** _____

⟶ **Day 3:** _____

Where to find these recipes: _____

_____

_____

(*Cookbook title with page #, recipe box, website, etc.*)

BEFORE SERVING

Reserve _____ for:

- ♦ _____
- ♦ _____

Chapter 4: Ground Turkey

Purchasing Ground Turkey

Ground turkey is very lean. Ground breast of turkey is 99 percent lean. I like the taste of both turkey breast, white meat, and ground leg and thigh, dark meat. Ground dark meat turkey has a higher percentage of fat, 10 - 15 percent, than white meat. That compares to 85 - 90 percent lean ground beef. For meat loaf, I like to use breast of turkey, but for soup, dark meat has more flavor. Ground turkey has a good flavor, but it's different from ground beef. You can substitute it in most recipes for ground beef by using spices and herbs that enhance the flavor. This chapter features recipes using ground turkey exclusively. The next chapter features a combination of ground turkey and ground beef.

Safe Handling

You can keep ground turkey in the refrigerator for 1 to 2 days. Cooked ground turkey keeps for 3 to 4 days. Cook ground turkey as you would regular turkey or chicken—to the temperature of 165 degrees F.

For more on information about ground turkey (and chicken), see the United States Department of Agriculture (USDA) link: http://www.fsis.usda.gov/Fact_Sheets/ground_poultry_and_food_safety/index.asp

Three-Day Plan

Day 1: Herbed Turkey Meatloaf ⤳ **Day 2:** Hearty Turkey-Vegetable Soup ⤳ **Day 3:** Easy Macaroni Skillet Dinner

Herbed Turkey Meatloaf

½ onion
2 pounds ground breast of turkey
2 eggs
½ cup ketchup
1 cup oat bran
2 tablespoons Worcestershire sauce
1 teaspoon prepared mustard
½ teaspoon sage
½ teaspoon marjoram
½ teaspoon celery salt
¼ teaspoon pepper

Preheat oven to 350 degrees F. Trim ends of onion; peel off outer skin. Grate onion into a large bowl, discarding root end. Add turkey, eggs, ketchup, oat bran, Worcestershire sauce, mustard, sage, marjoram, celery salt, and pepper.

Pour meat mixture into a shallow glass baking dish or into a glass 9x5x3-inch loaf pan. Form into a loaf. Bake for 1 hour 15 minutes, or until meat thermometer registers 160 degrees. Before serving, reserve half of meat loaf for next two recipes. Good served with baked potatoes and peas with pearl onions. Yield: 4 servings

BEFORE SERVING

Reserve half of the Herbed Turkey Meatloaf for:
- Hearty Turkey-Vegetable Soup
- Easy Macaroni Skillet Dinner

Hearty Turkey-Vegetable Soup

¼ small head cabbage
OR 1 cup shredded cabbage
Half of reserved Herbed Turkey Meatloaf (see previous page)
3 cups chicken broth
OR 3 cups water and 3 teaspoons chicken soup base
1 teaspoon salt
¼ teaspoon pepper
3 ribs celery
3 carrots
3 tablespoons rice
1 (8-oz.) can tomato sauce
1 (16-oz.) can diced tomatoes
1 (15-oz.) can red beans

Easy variation: Crumble and add reserved Herbed Turkey Meatloaf to 2 cans condensed vegetable soup and 2 cans water. Bring to a boil, stirring occasionally; serve.

Peel off loose, outer leaves of cabbage. Rinse under cold water. Cut in half lengthwise through the core to make 2 halves. Cut one half through the core to make two fourths. If there are bugs or dirt, soak cabbage in a bowl of salted water to cover for 15 minutes. (Refrigerate ¾ of cabbage to use in another recipe.) Place flat edge of ¼ of cabbage on a cutting board. Cut out core. Slice cabbage into ⅛-inch strips. Set aside.

Crumble reserved turkey meatloaf into a large pot. Add broth or water and soup base, salt, and pepper, and heat on medium. Rinse and trim leaves and ends of celery; cut in half crosswise. Cut lengthwise into strips; cut across strips to dice. Pare, rinse, and trim carrots; cut in half lengthwise, place flat side down, and cut into ¼-inch half circles.

Add cabbage, celery, carrots, rice, tomato sauce, and tomatoes to pot. Drain red beans in a colander, rinse, and add to the pot. Bring to a boil over high heat. Cover, turn down to low, and simmer 30 - 45 minutes or until carrots are cooked. Good served with toasted onion-rye bread and Swiss cheese. Yield: 4-6 servings

Easy Macaroni Skillet Dinner

1 onion
1 tablespoon oil
1 green pepper
Half of reserved Herbed Turkey Meatloaf (see page 64)
1 ½ cups uncooked macaroni
1 (16-oz.) can diced tomatoes with juice
1 (15-oz.) can corn with liquid
1 cup water
4 oz. Cheddar cheese, cubed
Salt and pepper to taste

Using a chef's knife, cut onion in half lengthwise on a cutting board. Peel off outer skin; cut out the root end. Place onion flat side down. Score; then cut to dice. Rinse and cut green pepper in half. Pull out and discard seeds. Slice into strips; then cut across strips to dice.

Heat oil in large skillet on medium. Sauté onion and pepper about 5 minutes, stirring occasionally. Crumble and add turkey meatloaf, macaroni, tomatoes, corn, and water. Bring to a boil over high heat; then turn down to low. Cover and simmer for half an hour, stirring occasionally. Sprinkle with cheese cubes, cover, and cook just until cheese melts, about 2 minutes. Add salt and pepper, if needed. Good served with broccoli salad. Yield: 4 servings

Chapter 5: Ground Turkey and Ground Beef

The Perfect Mixture

Ground turkey is lean and healthy. Ground beef adds flavor. Mix them together in equal parts for the following recipes. This is a great way to introduce ground turkey to your family.

Three-Day Plan

Day 1: Two-Meat Burritos ⟶ **Day 2:** Italian Pasta Skillet Dinner ⟶ **Day 3:** Spicy Tamale Pie

Two-Meat Burritos

2 onions
1 pound ground turkey
1 pound ground beef
2 teaspoons chili powder
2 tablespoons corn starch
2 cups beef broth
OR 2 cups water and 2 teaspoons beef soup base
1 cup grated Cheddar cheese
Bottled picante sauce
1 (8-count) package burrito-size flour tortillas

Using a chef's knife, cut onion in half on a cutting board. Peel off outer skin; cut out the root end. Score and dice; finely chop. Heat oil in large skillet on medium. Brown ground turkey, ground beef, and onion; break apart and turn using a large spatula. Drain grease. Add chili powder and cornstarch; stir to combine. Add broth or water and beef soup base, stirring until thickened. Turn down heat and let simmer 5 minutes. Before serving, reserve about half of the meat mixture for the next two meals.

Warm 4 tortillas by placing damp paper towels under and on top of flour tortillas on a plate. Heat in the microwave for about a minute or until warm. Repeat for second helpings Spoon meat filling onto flour tortilla; top with cheese and a picante sauce. Fold bottom edge up to keep filling in; then roll from left to right. Good served with refried beans and Spanish rice. Yield: 4 servings

BEFORE SERVING

Reserve half the meat mixture from Two-Meat Burritos for:
- Italian Pasta Skillet Dinner
- Spicy Tamale Pie

Italian Pasta Skillet Dinner

1 tablespoon chopped fresh parsley
OR 1 teaspoon dried parsley
2 teaspoons oil
2 cloves garlic
3 cups water
1 (16-oz.) can tomato sauce
½ teaspoon salt
¼ teaspoon oregano
¼ teaspoon basil
1 (8-oz.) package curly macaroni, uncooked
Half of reserved meat mixture from Two-Meat Burritos (see previous page)
2 tablespoons Parmesan cheese

For fresh parsley, place a small bunch in a colander and rinse under cold water. Rub the parsley with your fingers to remove dirt. Shake off excess water. Pat dry with a paper towel. Hold the parsley in a bunch and cut the leaves from the stems. Discard stems. Place leaves in a bowl and snip with kitchen shears or use a knife to chop on a cutting board. Set aside.

Heat oil in a large skillet on medium. Press the flat side of a chef's knife on the garlic cloves to break skin. Peel off skin. Trim off root end. Score; then cut to mince. Sauté garlic for two minutes; then add water, tomato sauce, parsley, salt, oregano, and basil. Bring to a boil; add macaroni and return to a boil. Cover and turn heat down to low. Simmer for 10 minutes, stirring occasionally. Add turkey/beef mixture and Parmesan cheese. Simmer uncovered 5 minutes more. Good served with spinach salad. Yield: 4 servings

Spicy Tamale Pie

Half of reserved meat mixture from Two-Meat Burritos (see page 67)
1 (16-oz.) can of tomatoes
1 (15-oz.) can of red beans
1 (16-oz.) can corn, drained
1 cup grated Cheddar cheese

Cornbread Topping:
1 cup flour
1 cup yellow cornmeal
1 teaspoon salt
1 teaspoon sugar
1 tablespoon baking powder
1 egg, beaten
1 cup milk
1 tablespoon oil

Preheat oven to 350 degrees F. Pour turkey/beef mixture into a 12x8x2-inch glass pan. Stir in tomatoes, beans, and corn. Top with cheese. In a medium-sized bowl, mix together flour, cornmeal, salt, sugar, baking powder, egg, milk, and oil. Pour over meat mixture. Bake for 45 - 60 minutes or until cornbread is golden-brown and cooked through. To serve, spoon cornbread onto plate and top with filling. Good served with a stir-fried zucchini. Yield: 4 servings

My Family Favorite Ground Turkey or Ground Turkey/Beef Mixture Three-Day Plan

Day 1: _____ ⟶ Day 2: _____

⟶ Day 3: _____

Where to find these recipes: _____

_____

_____

(*Cookbook title with page #, recipe box, website, etc.*)

BEFORE SERVING

Reserve _____ for:

- _____

- _____

Delicious Dinners with Beef

Chapter 6: Ground Beef

Purchase Ground Beef

Ground beef is made from the shoulder of the beef and other less tender cuts. Grinding beef helps to tenderize it. Fat improves the flavor. Ground beef is sold by naming the beef-to-fat ratio, such as 93 percent beef/7 percent fat, 85 percent beef/15 percent fat, 80 percent beef/20 percent fat, and 70 percent beef/30 percent fat. While 93 percent lean ground beef is healthier, I like to buy 85 percent. Fat adds flavor. Beef that is 93 percent lean is too lean to my taste, and 80 percent or less is too fatty.

Defrosting

If beef is frozen, defrost completely before you begin cooking. The best way to defrost beef is in the refrigerator, which takes about 1 day for ground beef, stew beef, and steaks. Roasts can take 2 days or longer depending on size. If you defrost beef on the counter, submerge it in a bowl of cold water and check every half hour. If the water is not cold, dump, and add cold water to the bowl. Once beef is defrosted, refrigerate until ready to cook. When defrosting beef in the microwave, cook it right away.

Drain Fat

After frying ground beef, I always drain the fat. To do this, move beef and vegetables to one side of the skillet using a large spatula. Tip the skillet slightly so fat drips to the opposite side. Spoon fat out of skillet to a mug or can to discard when cool. (To prevent clogged drains, never pour fat down the drain or into the garbage disposal.) After cooking hamburgers or other fatty foods, drain on a plate lined with paper towels.

For more information on ground beef, see the U.S. Department of Agriculture link::
http://www.fsis.usda.gov/Fact_Sheets/Ground_Beef_and_Food_Safety/index.asp

Three-Day Plan

Day 1: Betty's Spaghetti ⟶ **Day 2:** Quick 'n Easy Chili ⟶ **Day 3:** Kids' Fave Chili-Mac

Betty's Spaghetti

1 large onion
1 large green bell pepper
2 pounds ground beef
2 teaspoons oregano
½ teaspoon basil
2 (16-oz.) cans chopped tomatoes
2 (16-oz.) cans tomato sauce
2 (6-oz.) cans tomato paste
2 teaspoons sugar
1 (12-oz.) package whole-wheat spaghetti
Parmesan cheese

> Easy variation: Substitute two 32-oz. jars of pasta sauce for the sauce ingredients.

Cut onion in half lengthwise. Peel off outer skin; cut out the root end. Place onion flat side down. Score; then dice. Rinse and cut green pepper in half. Pull out and discard seeds. Cut into strips; then cut across strips to dice.

Fry ground beef, onion, and pepper in a large skillet over medium heat. Use a large spatula to turn and separate beef until cooked and brown. Drain fat. Add oregano and basil to meat mixture; stir. Pour into a large (4-quart) pot. Add tomatoes, tomato sauce, tomato paste, and sugar. Bring to a boil; turn heat to low. Cover and simmer for 15 - 30 minutes.

Cook pasta according to package directions; drain. Before serving, reserve half of sauce for the following two recipes. Ladle sauce over spaghetti. Pass Parmesan cheese at the table. Good served with mixed green salad and Italian garlic bread. Yield: 4 servings

BEFORE SERVING

Reserve half of Betty's Spaghetti sauce for:
- Quick 'n Easy Chili
- Kids' Fave Chili-Mac

Quick 'n Easy Chili

1 onion
1 tablespoon oil
All reserved sauce from Betty's Spaghetti (see previous page)
1 (15-oz.) can kidney beans
2 teaspoons chili powder
1 teaspoon cumin
½ teaspoon cayenne pepper (optional)
½ teaspoon salt
1 cup grated Cheddar cheese

Cut onion in half lengthwise. Peel off outer skin; cut out the root end. Place onion flat side down. Score; then dice. Heat oil in a large (4-quart) pot on medium. Sauté onion for 5 - 10 minutes or until translucent. Add reserved spaghetti sauce. Drain and rinse kidney beans in a colander; add to pot. Add water, chili powder, and cumin. Add cayenne pepper if you like hot, spicy chili.

Bring to a boil over medium-high heat. Cover and turn down heat to very low. Let simmer about 15 minutes to blend flavors. Before serving, reserve about ¼ of the chili (2 - 3 cups) for tomorrow night's meal, Kids' Fave Chili-Mac. Ladle chili into bowls and sprinkle Cheddar cheese on top. Good served with cornbread muffins. Yield: 4 servings

BEFORE SERVING
Reserve about ¼ of Quick 'n Easy Chili for:
- Kids' Fave Chili-Mac

Kids' Fave Chili-Mac

1 (8-oz.) package whole-grain elbow macaroni
2 tablespoons butter or margarine, divided
2 tablespoons flour
1 cup milk
1 cup grated Cheddar cheese
Reserved chili (2 - 3 cups) from Quick 'n Easy Chili (see previous page)
¼ cup whole-bread crumbs
2 tablespoons Parmesan cheese

Preheat oven to 350 degrees F. Cook macaroni according to package directions. Meanwhile, melt butter or margarine in a medium-sized (3-quart) saucepan over medium heat. Add flour; cook and stir 1 minute. Whisk in milk, stirring frequently until thickened. Add cheese, stirring until melted. Stir in cooked and drained macaroni and reserved chili.

Grease a 2-quart casserole dish. Pour in chili-macaroni mixture using a rubber spatula to scrape the sides. Sprinkle on breadcrumbs and Parmesan cheese. Bake until hot and bubbly, about 20 minutes. Good served with steamed broccoli. Yield: 4 servings

Easy variation: Substitute a family-size box of macaroni and cheese for the homemade recipe. Prepare according to package directions. Then mix with the reserved chili and bake as above.

Three-Day Plan

Day 1: Summer Day Cheeseburgers ⟶ **Day 2:** Cheeseburger Soup ⟶ **Day 3:** Stacked Enchiladas con Huevos

Summer Day Cheeseburgers

2 pounds ground beef
1 egg
1 tablespoon dried minced onion
1 tomato
1 red onion
4 lettuce leaves
4 hamburger buns
4 slices American cheese
Salt and pepper to taste
Ketchup
Mustard
Dill pickle slices

Heat barbeque grill on medium-high. Mix beef, egg, and onion. Form 8 beef patties, each ¼ pound of beef. Grill over medium-high heat for about 5 minutes to sear in flavor, flip over, and turn down heat to medium. Cook until done, about 10 minutes total, depending on the thickness of the burger. Burgers should be cooked through with no pink, 160 degrees F. on a meat thermometer.

To cook indoors, move oven rack to upper position so that burgers can cook about 4 inches from the heating element. Preheat oven broiler. Place patties on broiler pan and position under broiler. Broil about 5 minutes, flip over and broil an additional 5 minutes.

Meanwhile, rinse, trim core and end, and slice tomato. Trim ends, peel skin, and slice red onion. Rinse lettuce and spin or pat dry. Toast buns. To melt cheese, place 1 slice of cheese each on 4 of the burgers the last few minutes of cooking. Remove from heat. Reserve 4 burgers for the next 2 meals.

Place one cheeseburger on each of the 4 buns. Sprinkle with salt and pepper. Top with ketchup, mustard, pickle, tomato, onion, and lettuce. Good served with corn on the cob and fresh fruit. Yield: 4 servings

BEFORE SERVING
Reserve 4 of the hamburgers for:
- Cheeseburger Soup
- Stacked Enchiladas con Huevos

Cheeseburger Soup

1 onion
2 ribs celery
1 (15-oz.) can corn
1 (10-oz.) can diced tomatoes with green chili peppers
12 slices (8-oz.) American cheese
3 cups chicken broth
OR 3 cups water and 3 teaspoons chicken soup base
2 reserved hamburgers from Summer Day Cheeseburger recipe (see previous page)
¼ cup water
2 tablespoons corn starch

Using a chef's knife, cut onion in half lengthwise on a cutting board. Peel off outer skin; cut out the root end. Place onion flat side down. Score; then cut to dice. Rinse and trim leaves and ends of celery; cut in half crosswise. Slice celery into strips; then cut across strips to dice.

Heat oil in large pot over medium heat. Add onion and celery. Sauté about 5 minutes or until crisp-tender. Add corn, undrained, and tomatoes with juice. Cut or tear American cheese and add to pot. Stir in broth or water and soup base. Bring to a boil over high heat, turn down to low, cover, and simmer for 30 minutes.

Cut or crumble hamburger and add to soup. Mix water and cornstarch in a small bowl with a fork. Add to soup while stirring. Simmer an additional 2 minutes until thickened and bubbly. Good served with corn tortilla chips and dill pickles. Yield: 4 servings

Stacked Enchiladas con Huevos

Approximately ½ cup oil
12 corn tortillas
1 (15-oz.) can mild enchilada sauce
1 onion
2 reserved hamburgers from Summer Day Cheeseburgers (see page 76)
1½ cups grated Monterey-Jack cheese
4 eggs

Pour a thin layer of oil into a skillet. Reserve the rest of the oil to add as needed. Heat oil on medium. Fry corn tortillas, one at a time, for about 30 seconds or until they blister; turn and fry a few seconds on the other side. Remove from skillet onto plate lined with paper towels. Tortillas will be pliable, not hard or crisp. Repeat until all tortillas are fried. (Set aside skillet to fry eggs just before serving.) Pour enchilada sauce in a second skillet or pan wide enough to dip tortillas and heat on medium-low. Meanwhile, cut onion in half on a cutting board using a chef's knife. Peel off outer skin; cut out the root end. Score and finely chop onion.

Preheat oven to 325 degrees F. Dip a tortilla in the enchilada sauce and place in a glass pan or casserole dish. (Allow enough room to place four tortillas flat in the pan, using 2 pans if necessary.) Cut hamburgers into fourths. Crumble one fourth of the hamburger on top of tortilla. Sprinkle on about a teaspoon of onion and a tablespoon of cheese. Dip and stack a second tortilla on top of first tortilla, crumble on one fourth of the hamburger, sprinkle with onion, and cheese. Dip and stack a third tortilla. On top layer, sprinkle only with onion and cheese (no beef) to complete triple-layer, stacked enchilada. Repeat process to make 4 total, triple-layer, stacked enchiladas.

Cover with foil. Bake for 15-20 minutes or until enchiladas are hot and cheese is melted. After about 15 minutes, heat oil in skillet reserved from frying tortillas on medium-low. Crack eggs into hot oil gently so yolks will not break. When egg whites turn from clear to white and are nearly set, carefully turn over with a spatula. Fry a minute more. Use a wide spatula to transfer enchiladas to plates. Place a fried egg on top. Good served with guacamole, shredded lettuce, and diced tomato.
Yield: 4 servings

Three-Day Plan

Day 1: Crispy Tacos ⟶ **Day 2:** Beef-Barley Soup ⟶ **Day 3:** Kids' Choice Sloppy Joes

Crispy Tacos

¼ head iceberg lettuce
1 onion
2 pounds ground beef
½ teaspoon chili powder
½ teaspoon paprika
½ teaspoon cumin
¼ teaspoon garlic powder
1 teaspoon cornstarch
½ cup water
1 (10-count) package hard taco shells
1 tomato
1 cup grated Cheddar cheese
Bottled salsa

Wash lettuce first or earlier in the day to let water drain. Cut out core or rap core on counter hard enough to break it loose. Discard core. Turn lettuce head upside down and run under cold water, allowing the water to push apart leaves and flow into the lettuce head. Turn core side down and place in a colander to drain. To shred, slice thinly using a chef's knife.

Use a cutting board; cut onion in half. Peel off outer skin; cut out the root end. Score and dice onion. Brown ground beef and onion in large skillet over medium heat. Turn stove off. Drain grease. Reserve three-fourths (1½ pounds) of the cooked beef/onion mixture for the next 2 recipes.

Over medium heat, stir seasoning with remaining beef in skillet: chili powder, paprika, cumin, garlic powder, and cornstarch. Add water, stirring until thickened. Turn down heat to low, cover, and simmer 5 minutes to blend flavors.

Preheat oven to 325 degrees F. Meanwhile, rinse, core, trim ends, and dice tomato.

Place taco shells on an ungreased cookie sheet, slightly overlapping, and heat until warm, about 6 minutes or according to package directions. Serve tacos family style with bowls of beef mixture, salsa, tomatoes, lettuce, and cheese passed at the table. Fill taco shells with about a spoonful of meat, salsa, tomatoes, lettuce, and cheese. Good served with Spanish rice and refried beans. Yield: 4 servings

BEFORE SERVING

Reserve about ¾ (1 ½ pounds) of the cooked ground beef/onion mixture from Crispy Tacos for:
- Beef-Barley Soup
- Kids' Choice Sloppy Joes

Beef-Barley Soup

1 small onion
1 rib celery
1 carrot
2 tablespoons oil
6 - 7 cups beef broth, divided
OR 6 - 7 cups water and 7 teaspoons beef soup base, divided
1 cup medium barley
1 can (16 oz.) stewed tomatoes
1 tablespoon chopped fresh parsley
OR 1 teaspoon dried parsley
Half of (¾ pound) reserved cooked ground beef/onion mixture from Crispy Taco recipe (see page 80)

Use a chef's knife to cut onion in half on a cutting board. Peel off outer skin; cut out the root end. Score and dice onion. Rinse and trim leaves and ends of celery; cut in half crosswise and then into sticks. To dice, cut sticks crosswise. Pare, rinse, and trim carrot; cut in half crosswise. Make a flat edge by slicing a thin lengthwise piece so carrot won't roll. Cut carrot lengthwise into slices. Then cut slices lengthwise into sticks; cut crosswise to dice.

Heat oil on medium in a large (4-quart) pot. Add onion, celery, and carrots and sauté about 10 minutes until softened, stirring occasionally. Add 6 cups broth or water and soup base, barley, and stewed tomatoes with juice. Bring to a boil over high heat; reduce to low, cover, and simmer 1 hour.

Add reserved beef and additional cup of broth if barley has absorbed most of the broth. Simmer 5 minutes.

For fresh parsley, place a small bunch in a colander and rinse under cold water. Rub the parsley with your fingers to remove dirt. Shake off excess water. Pat dry with a paper towel. Hold the parsley in a bunch and cut the leaves from the stems. Discard stems. Place leaves in a bowl and snip with kitchen shears or use a knife to chop on a cutting board. Stir in parsley. Good served with rye crackers and butter. Yield: 4 - 6 servings

Kids' Choice Sloppy Joes

1 tablespoon oil
2 ribs celery
1 small green bell pepper
Half of reserved (¾ pound) cooked ground beef/onion mixture from Crispy Taco recipe (see page 80)
3 tablespoons Worcestershire sauce
½ cup (4 oz.) tomato sauce
2 teaspoons sugar
1 teaspoon vinegar
½ teaspoon hot pepper sauce
½ teaspoon salt
¾ cup water
4 hamburger buns

Rinse and trim celery leaves and ends; cut in half crosswise on a cutting board. Cut celery lengthwise into sticks, then crosswise to dice; finely chop. Rinse and cut green pepper in half. Pull out and discard seeds. Slice into strips, cut strips crosswise to dice, and finely chop.

Heat oil in a skillet on medium. Sauté celery and green pepper for about 5 minutes, stirring frequently. Add beef/onion mixture, Worcestershire sauce, tomato sauce, sugar, vinegar, pepper sauce, salt, and water. Bring to a boil. Turn down heat to very low, cover, and simmer for 30 minutes, stirring occasionally. Remove lid and simmer 5 minutes more to thicken sauce. To serve, heap meat mixture onto buns. Good served with corn on the cob and baked beans. Yield: 4 servings

Three-Day Plan

Day 1: Salisbury Steak with Mushroom Sauce → **Day 2:** Super Nachos → **Day 3:** Hearty Corn Stew

Salisbury Steak with Mushroom Sauce

2 pounds ground beef
1 onion
2 eggs
¼ cup dry breadcrumbs
1 tablespoon soy sauce
½ teaspoon salt
½ teaspoon pepper
3 tablespoons butter or margarine, divided
2 tablespoons oil, divided
6 ounces (about 8) button mushrooms
¼ cup flour
2 cups beef broth
OR 2 cups water and 2 teaspoons beef soup base
1 tablespoon red wine
Salt and pepper to taste

Place ground beef into a large bowl. Using a chef's knife, cut onion in half lengthwise on a cutting board. Peel off outer skin; cut out the root end. Grate onion and add to beef, along with eggs, breadcrumbs, and soy sauce. Form 8 (1-inch thick) oval patties and place on a broiler pan about 1 inch apart. Broil 4 inches from heat for 6 - 7 minutes on each side or until well done. Remove broiler pan from oven. Reserve 4 Salisbury Steaks for the next two meals.

Meanwhile, place mushrooms in a bowl of cold water. Stir with hands; dirt will fall to the bottom of the bowl. Do not let soak as they will absorb water. Remove mushrooms from water, and place on a cutting board. Pat dry with a paper towel. Slice about ¼ inch thick. Heat 1 tablespoon butter or margarine and 1 tablespoon oil in a large skillet on medium/medium-high. Sauté mushrooms, stirring constantly, for about 3 minutes, until brown and slightly smaller in size. Pour mushrooms into a bowl and set aside. `

Turn down heat to medium. Add 2 tablespoons butter or margarine and 1 tablespoon oil to skillet. Add flour to skillet; stir frequently until flour is light brown. Whisk in beef broth or water and soup base, stirring until thickened and bubbly. Turn down heat to low. Add wine. Taste; season with salt and pepper if needed. If Salisbury Steaks have cooled, add to skillet, cover and heat for about 2 - 4 minutes on low or until heated through. Drain mushrooms and add to skillet. Place Salisbury Steaks on dinner plates and ladle mushroom sauce to cover. Good served with mashed potatoes and green beans with slivered almonds. Yield: 4 servings

BEFORE SERVING

Reserve 4 Salisbury Steaks for:
- Super Nachos
- Hearty Corn Stew

Super Nachos

1 (15-oz.) can diced, stewed tomatoes
1 (16-oz.) package sliced American cheese
1 green bell pepper
1 spicy pepper such as jalapeno
1 teaspoon hot pepper sauce
2 reserved Salisbury Steaks (see previous page)
1 (16-oz.) package tortilla chips

Pour tomatoes and juice into a medium-sized (2-quart) saucepan. Dice or tear cheese and mix it with tomatoes. Heat on medium-low until cheese is melted, stirring frequently. Rinse and cut bell pepper in half. Pull out and discard seeds. Slice into strips; then cut across strips to dice. To cut spicy pepper, wear gloves and follow the same process as bell pepper. Add peppers to cheese mixture. Crumble and add Salisbury Steaks. Heat for about 3 minutes until steak is warm. Serve over tortilla chips. Good with fried potatoes and bean dip.

Easy variation: Substitute 1 (4-oz.) can chopped green chilies for bell and spicy peppers.

Hearty Corn Stew

1 large onion
1 red bell pepper
1 green bell pepper
6 ribs celery
3 tablespoons oil
2 tablespoons flour
1 (46-oz.) can tomato juice
1 (15-oz.) can corn
2 teaspoons sugar
2 reserved Salisbury Steaks (see page 84)
Salt and pepper to taste

Use a chef's knife to cut onion in half lengthwise on a cutting board. Peel off outer skin; cut out the root end. Place onion flat side down. Score, dice, and chop fine. Rinse red and green peppers and cut in half. Pull out and discard seeds. Slice into strips; then cut across strips to dice. Rinse and trim leaves and ends of celery; cut in half crosswise. Cut lengthwise into sticks, then crosswise to dice.

Heat oil on medium 4-quart pot. Sauté onion, pepper, and celery about 10 minutes until onion is translucent. Stir in flour. Add tomato juice and corn with liquid. Heat on high to boiling; then turn down to low. Cover and simmer about 20 minutes. Add sugar. Crumble and add Salisbury Steaks. Heat to boiling. Turn heat to low and simmer 2 - 4 minutes. Add salt and pepper to taste. Good served with Italian garlic bread. Yield: 4 servings

Three-Day Plan

Day 1: Pizza Rounds ⟶ **Day 2:** Oodles of Noodles Casserole ⟶ **Day 3:** Kansas City Steak Soup

Pizza Rounds

2 pounds ground beef
1 (8-oz.) can tomato sauce
½ cup grated mozzarella cheese
2 (8-oz.) tubes refrigerated crescent rolls (16 rolls total)

Preheat oven to 375 degrees F. Brown ground beef in a large skillet over medium heat. Use a large spatula to turn and separate beef until cooked and brown. Drain fat. Reserve ¾ (1 ½ pounds) of beef for next two meals. Add tomato sauce and cheese to skillet. Mix well.

Grease two baking sheets. Unroll crescent dough on prepared cookie sheets. Pinch seams of two triangles together to make eight rectangles. Divide meat-cheese mixture among dough, placing mixture down the center of the rectangles. Enclose meat mixture inside of dough, pinching dough to make eight rolls. Cut each roll into three pieces. Place pieces seam-side down, spacing them 2 inches apart on baking sheets.

Bake for 15 minutes. Good served with tossed salad and fresh vegetables, such as baby carrots, celery sticks, and broccoli florets, and creamy Ranch dip. Yield: 24 rounds

BEFORE SERVING

Reserve ¾ of the ground beef (about 1½ pounds) from Pizza Rounds for:
- Oodles of Noodles Casserole
- Kansas City Steak Soup

Oodles of Noodles Casserole

2 green onions
1 (8-oz.) package noodles
1 cup cottage cheese
1 cup sour cream
Half of the reserved beef from Pizza Rounds (see previous page)
½ teaspoon salt
⅛ teaspoon pepper
¼ teaspoon garlic salt
1 (8-oz.) can tomato sauce
1 cup grated sharp Cheddar cheese

Preheat oven to 350 degrees F. Grease a 2-quart casserole dish. Rinse green onions. Trim top and root end, and remove loose outer skin. Cut crosswise, starting with green top, into ⅛-inch circles. Cook noodles according to package directions; drain in colander and rinse in cold water. Pour noodles into a large bowl. Stir in green onions, cottage cheese, and sour cream.

Mix beef, salt, pepper, garlic salt, and tomato sauce in a separate bowl. Pour half of noodle mixture into prepared casserole dish. Spoon half of meat mixture over noodles; repeat. Top with Cheddar cheese. Bake for 40 - 45 minutes or until cheese is melted and lightly browned. Good served with spinach. Yield: 4 servings

Kansas City Steak Soup

1 onion
2 carrots
2 ribs celery
1 garlic clove
2 tablespoons oil
Half of the reserved beef from Pizza Rounds (see page 88)
1 (8-oz.) can tomato sauce
5 cups beef broth
OR 5 cups water and 5 teaspoons beef soup base
1 tablespoon Worcestershire sauce
½ teaspoon hot pepper sauce
¼ teaspoon freshly ground pepper
2 tablespoons butter or margarine
¼ cup flour

Using a chef's knife, cut onion in half lengthwise on a cutting board. Peel off outer skin; cut out the root end. Place onion flat side down. Score; then cut to dice. Pare, rinse, and trim ends of carrots; cut in half crosswise. To prevent carrot from rolling, cut a flat edge, lengthwise. Cut lengthwise into slices. Then cut slices lengthwise into sticks; cut crosswise to dice. Rinse and trim leaves and ends of celery; cut in half crosswise. Cut lengthwise into sticks, then crosswise to dice. Press the flat side of a chef's knife on garlic clove to break skin. Peel off skin. Trim off root end. Score; then cut to mince. Heat oil in a large (4-quart) pot on medium. Add onion, carrots, celery, and garlic and cook, stirring occasionally, about 10 minutes until softened.

Add beef, tomato sauce, broth or water and soup base, Worcestershire sauce, pepper sauce, and ground pepper. Bring to a boil over high heat; turn down to low, cover and simmer 15 minutes. Meanwhile, melt butter or margarine in a small saucepan over medium heat. Add flour and cook, stirring constantly, until light brown. To prevent lumps, whisk flour mixture into soup; cover and simmer an additional 15 minutes. Good served with oatmeal bread. Yield: 4 servings

Three-Day Plan

Day 1: Mexican Lasagna ⟶ **Day 2:** Grandma Lil's Stuffed Cabbage ⟶ **Day 3:** Main Dish Taco Salad

Mexican Lasagna

2 pounds ground beef
1 teaspoon chili powder
½ teaspoon cumin
½ teaspoon paprika
¼ teaspoon garlic powder
Dash cayenne pepper
1 (15-oz.) can whole kernel corn
1 cup bottled salsa
1 (15-oz.) can tomato sauce
1 (16-oz.) carton small-curd cottage cheese
2 eggs
1 teaspoon oregano
1 (10-count) package flour tortillas
1½ cups grated Monterey Jack cheese

Preheat oven to 375 degrees F. Cook beef in a skillet over medium heat. Use a spatula to break apart and turn until all meat is browned; drain grease. Spoon about three-fourths of the drained beef (1½ pounds) into a container and refrigerate for the next two meals. Keep remaining (½ pound) beef in the skillet.

Add chili powder, cumin, paprika, garlic powder, cayenne pepper, drained corn, salsa, and tomato sauce to skillet. Bring to boil over high heat; turn to low and simmer, stirring frequently, for 5 minutes. In a separate bowl, combine cottage cheese, eggs, and oregano.

Grease a 13x9x2-inch glass baking dish. Line bottom of baking dish with 5 tortillas, overlapping edges. Top with half the meat mixture. Spoon and spread all the cottage cheese mixture over meat. Arrange 5 tortillas over cheese mixture. Spread with remaining meat mixture. Top with Monterey Jack cheese. Bake for 30 minutes until hot and bubbly. Let stand for 5 minutes before serving. Good served with a mixed green salad. Yield: 4 servings

> ## BEFORE SERVING
> Reserve three-fourths of ground beef (1 ½ -pounds) from Mexican Lasagna for:
> - Grandma Lil's Stuffed Cabbage
> - Main Dish Taco Salad

Grandma Lil's Stuffed Cabbage

1 (3-pound) head of cabbage
1 onion
⅔ of reserved ground beef (about a pound) from Mexican Lasagna (see previous page)
1 cup uncooked rice
1 egg
½ teaspoon salt
¼ teaspoon pepper
1 (26-oz.) jar pasta sauce
1 tablespoon lemon juice

Trim a small slice off of the core end of the cabbage. Peel off the loose, outer leaves and discard. Rinse under cold water. Fill a large (6 - 8-quart) pot with 1 inch water; bring to a boil over high heat. Add cabbage, cover, turn down heat to medium, and simmer for 15 minutes. Let cabbage cool while you make the filling.

Trim the ends of the onion; peel off outer skin. Grate onion into a large bowl. Stir in beef, uncooked rice, egg, salt, and pepper. Remove cabbage from pot and discard water. Add about one third of the pasta sauce to the pot. Peel a leaf from cabbage head and place on a dinner plate. Scoop about two heaping tablespoons of the meat mixture onto the cabbage leaf. Fold in the leaf on four sides to conceal the mixture.

Place the cabbage roll in the pot on top of the pasta sauce, folded side down.

Repeat process of filling cabbage leaves with meat mixture to make cabbage rolls. Add pasta sauce in between layers. Add lemon juice to pot. Bring to a boil; then turn down heat to very low. Simmer for 1½ hours to 2 hours, or bake for about 2 hours in oven at 325 degree F. Good served with mashed potatoes. Yield: 6 - 8 servings

Main Dish Taco Salad

1 tomato
1 head green leaf lettuce
1 (15-oz.) can kidney beans
⅓ of reserved ground beef (½ pound) from Mexican Lasagna (see page 91)
1 teaspoon chili powder
1 tablespoon corn starch
½ cup beef broth
OR ½ cup water and ½ teaspoon beef soup base
1 cup grated Cheddar cheese
1 (12-oz.) bag tortilla chips
Bottled salsa
Bottled Ranch salad dressing

Rinse, trim end, core, and dice tomato. Place in a serving bowl. Tear lettuce into pieces and place in a large bowl and cover with cold water. Use your hand to stir the lettuce so dirt can fall to the bottom. Gather the lettuce, carrying it up out of the water and into salad spinner basket, rotating to dry (or pat dry with towels).

Drain kidney beans in a colander; rinse. Heat kidney beans, ground beef, chili powder, cornstarch, and beef broth or water and soup base in a saucepan on medium, stirring occasionally until thickened. Turn down heat to low, cover, and simmer 5 minutes.

Serve taco salad family style. Pass lettuce, beef/bean mixture, cheese, tortilla chips, salsa, tomato, and salad dressing at the table. Good served with avocado. Yield: 4 servings

Three-Day Plan

Day 1: Meatball Heroes ⟶ **Day 2:** Easy Lasagna ⟶ **Day 3:** Meatball Stew

Meatball Heroes

2 pounds ground beef
1 cup dry breadcrumbs
¼ cup grated Parmesan cheese
2 eggs
2 teaspoons salt
Dash pepper
½ teaspoon dried minced onion
½ cup cold water
2 tablespoons oil
1 (16-oz.) jar pasta sauce
4 submarine sandwich rolls
1 cup grated mozzarella cheese

Mix ground beef, breadcrumbs, Parmesan cheese, eggs, salt, pepper, onion, and water in a large bowl. Roll into small balls, ½ - 1 inch. Heat oil in a large skillet over medium heat. Cook meatballs in batches; do not crowd pan. Brown on all both sides, about 10 minutes total. Add more oil if needed. Remove to a paper towel-lined plate to drain.

Reserve two-thirds of the meatballs for the next two recipes. Heat spaghetti sauce and meatballs in a large saucepan over medium-low heat. Split rolls in half; toast. Spoon meatballs and sauce onto rolls. Sprinkle on cheese. Place under broiler for a minute to melt cheese. Good served with three-bean salad. Yield: 4 servings

BEFORE SERVING

Reserve ⅔ of the meatballs from Meatball Heroes for:
- Easy Lasagna
- Meatball Stew

Easy Lasagna

1 cup ricotta cheese
2 cups grated mozzarella cheese, divided
¼ cup grated Parmesan cheese
1 egg
½ teaspoon dried parsley
½ teaspoon salt
1 (24-oz.) jar pasta sauce
1 (9-oz.) package no-boil lasagna noodles
Half of the reserved meatballs from Meatball Heroes (see previous page)

Preheat oven to 350 degrees F. In a medium-sized bowl, mix ricotta cheese, 1½ cups mozzarella cheese, Parmesan cheese, egg, parsley, and salt.

In an 8x8x2-inch glass pan, spoon about 1 cup pasta sauce. Arrange 2 (uncooked) lasagna noodles over sauce. Spread ½ of cheese mixture over noodles, then ½ of the meatballs, and about 1 cup sauce. Repeat, layering noodles, cheese, meatballs, and sauce. Top with noodles (you will not need the whole box) for a total of 3 layers and remaining sauce.

Cover with foil. Bake 45 minutes or until hot and bubbly. Remove foil, sprinkle with remaining ½ cup mozzarella cheese, and bake 5 more minutes. Let stand 5 minutes before serving. Good served with a mixed green salad. Yield: 4 servings

Meatball Stew

1 onion
3 ribs celery
3 carrots
2 tablespoons oil
2 tablespoons flour
3 red potatoes
1 cup beef broth
Or 1 cup water and 1 teaspoon beef soup base
½ cup red wine
1 (16-oz.) can chopped tomatoes
1 tablespoon sugar
½ teaspoon basil
Half of reserved meatballs from Meatball Heroes (see page 95)

Use a chef's knife to cut onion in half on cutting board. Peel off outer skin; cut out the root end. Score and dice onion. Rinse and trim leaves and ends of celery; cut in half crosswise and then into sticks. To dice, cut sticks crosswise. Pare, rinse, and trim ends of carrots; cut in half, lengthwise. Place carrots flat side down and cut crosswise into ½-inch half circles. Heat oil in a large (4-quart) pot on medium. Add onions, celery, and carrots and sauté about 10 minutes until softened. Add flour, stirring to combine.

Meanwhile, pare and rinse potatoes. Using a cutting board, cut in ½-inch slices; then cut crosswise to dice. Add potatoes to pot, along with beef broth or water and soup base, wine, tomatoes with juice, sugar, and basil. Bring to a boil over high heat; turn down to lowest setting. Cover and simmer 45 minutes. Add meatballs and simmer an additional 15 minutes. Good served with Dilly bread. Yield: 4 servings

My Family Favorite Ground Beef Three-Day Plan

Day 1: _____ ⤳ **Day 2:** _____

⤳ **Day 3:** _____

Where to find these recipes: _____

_____

_____

(*Cookbook title with page #, recipe box, website, etc.*)

BEFORE SERVING

Reserve _____ for:

- ♦ _____

- ♦ _____

98 *Mealtime Magic*

Chapter 7: Beef Stews

Stew beef is cut into cubes from a tough part of the beef such as the shoulder. Cooking stew beef in moist heat for a few hours helps to tenderize it. Stew beef is seared first to keep in the juices and then simmered in broth for 3 hours. Less tender cuts have advantages. They cost less, are lower in fat, and are very flavorful.

For more on information about beef, see the United States Department of Agriculture (USDA) link: http://www.fsis.usda.gov/Factsheets/Beef_from_Farm_to_Table/index.asp

Three-Day Plan

Day 1: Classic Beef Stew with Wine ⟶ **Day 2:** Shepherd's Pie ⟶ **Day 3:** Quick & Easy Beef and Noodles

Classic Beef Stew with Wine

4 tablespoons oil, divided
½ cup flour, approximately
2 teaspoons oregano leaves
2 pounds stew beef
6 cups beef broth
OR 6 cups water and 6 teaspoons beef soup base
1 cup red wine, such as Burgundy
1 (8-oz.) can tomato sauce
1 onion
8 carrots
8 ribs celery
4 red potatoes
2 tablespoons cornstarch
¼ cup water

Heat 2 tablespoons oil in a large skillet over medium heat. Pour flour onto wax paper or a dinner plate; mix in oregano. Dredge about a fourth of the beef stew meat in flour mixture; pat to remove excess flour. Add to skillet, but do not crowd pan, or beef will steam instead of searing in juices. Sauté, turning to brown all sides, about 5 minutes. Remove from skillet to large (6 - 8-quart) pot. Add 1 tablespoon oil to skillet and repeat process (dredge in flour, add to skillet, sauté, and remove to soup pot) until all beef stew meat is seared. Add more oil to skillet, if needed.

Add ½ cup of the broth or water (no need to add soup base for this step) to skillet to deglaze (dissolve the bits of meat stuck to the pan) the pan, stirring, to loosen the flavorful, burnt-on pieces. Pour into soup pot, along with remaining broth or water and soup base, wine, and tomato sauce. Using a cutting board, trim end of onion. Peel off outer skin of onion, leaving on root end. Add onion, whole, to soup pot to flavor stew. Bring to a boil over high heat; turn down to lowest setting. Cover and simmer 2 hours.

Pare, rinse, and trim ends of carrots; cut in half crosswise. Cut in half lengthwise. Place flat side down; then cut crosswise into ½-inch half circles. Rinse and trim leaves and ends of celery. Cut celery in half crosswise. Line up celery to make ends even, and cut crosswise into 1-inch pieces. Pare and rinse potatoes. Cut in half, then into fourths.

Add carrots, celery, and potatoes to pot. Bring to a boil; then turn down to low. Simmer one more hour, until vegetables and meat are tender. Discard onion. Mix cornstarch and water in a small bowl or cup. Stir into soup. Let simmer a few minutes more. Serve beef stew in bowls. Serve all the potatoes because they are not needed in the next two recipes. Reserve about half of the beef stew, including about half of the carrots and celery, for the next two meals. Good served with crusty bread for dipping into gravy. Yield: 4 servings

BEFORE SERVING

Reserve half of the beef stew, carrots, and celery from Classic Beef Stew with Wine for:
- Shepherd's Pie
- Quick & Easy Beef and Noodles

Shepherd's Pie

4 medium-sized, red potatoes
½ of reserved Classic Beef Stew with Wine (see page 99)
1 cup frozen peas
1 tablespoon butter or margarine
Water reserved from cooking potatoes
¼ cup milk
Salt and pepper to taste
1 teaspoon parsley

Pare and rinse potatoes. Using a cutting board, cut in ½-inch slices; then cut crosswise to dice. Place in a large (3 - 4-quart) pot. Add water just to cover potatoes. Bring to a boil over high heat; then turn down to medium-low, cover, and simmer for 15 minutes or until soft.

Preheat oven to 375 degrees F. Using a slotted spoon, scoop about half of reserved beef, carrots, and celery into an 8x8-inch glass baking dish or 2-quart casserole. Stir in peas. Ladle a few spoonfuls of gravy over the meat and vegetables to moisten.

When potatoes are cooked, pour off water from potatoes, reserving about ¼ cup to use for mashing. Mix this hot water and milk; set aside. Add butter or margarine to potatoes and lightly sprinkle with salt and pepper. Puree potatoes with a potato masher. Gradually stir in the milk mixture to desired consistency to make fluffy mashed potatoes. Spoon and spread mashed potatoes over beef and vegetables.

Bake for 30 - 40 minutes or until potatoes are hot and bubbly. Sprinkle with parsley. Good served with warm whole-wheat rolls and butter. Yield: 4 servings

Quick & Easy Beef and Noodles

2 quarts water
1 teaspoon salt
1 (12-oz.) package frozen, home-style egg noodles
½ of reserved Classic Beef Stew with Wine (see page 99)

Pour water into a medium-large (4-quart) pot. Add salt and bring to a boil over high heat; add noodles. Return to a boil; then turn down heat to medium-high and simmer uncovered for 20 minutes or until noodles are cooked. Drain and place back in pot. Add reserved beef stew, bring to a simmer, and turn down heat to low. Simmer 5 minutes until stew is hot. Good served with a mixed green salad. Yield: 4 servings

My Family Favorite Beef Stew Three-Day Plan

Day 1: _____ ↗ **Day 2:** _____

↗ **Day 3:** _____

Where to find these recipes: _____

_____

_____

(*Cookbook title with page #, recipe box, website, etc.*)

BEFORE SERVING

Reserve _____ for:

- _____

- _____

Chapter 8: Beef Steaks

Steaks should be well-marbled, meaning fat should be distributed throughout the steak to make it tender. Steaks should be cooked with dry heat, such as grilling or broiling. For moist, tender steaks, cook rare, medium-rare, or medium. If steaks are cooked well done, they can dry out and become tough. Cooking time for steaks is short.

Three-Day Plan

Day 1: Steak Supreme ⟶ **Day 2:** Steak and Tomato Salad ⟶ **Day 3:** Steak Fajitas

Steak Supreme

2 pounds steak, such as Kansas City strip, T-bone, Porterhouse, or filet mignon
1 large onion
1 (8-oz.) package button mushrooms
2 tablespoon oil, divided
1 tablespoon butter or margarine
Salt and pepper to taste

To cook outdoors, fire up coals or heat gas grill to medium. To grill steak, sear it over medium-high heat on both sides to begin; then turn heat to medium to cook to desired doneness. To prevent tough, dry steak, do not overcook, and salt and pepper only after cooking. Total cooking time depends on the thickness of the steak and the desired doneness, approximately 15 minutes total.

To cook indoors, move oven rack to upper position so that steaks can cook about 3 inches from the heating element. Preheat oven broiler. Place steaks on broiler pan and position under broiler. Broil 5 - 8 minutes; flip over and broil an additional 5 - 8 minutes. Frying steaks is an alternative indoor cooking, but instead of a skillet, use a griddle.

A griddle is better for cooking steaks than a skillet because it has no sides, which causes steaming. Heat oil on griddle on medium-high. Sear steak for about 3 minutes; turn and sear other side. Turn heat to medium or medium-low and cook for 5-7 minutes on each side until desired doneness, depending on thickness.

Meanwhile, prepare the vegetables. Using a chef's knife, cut onion in half on a cutting board. Peel off outer skin; cut out the root end. Cut onion into thin slices. Place mushrooms in a bowl of cool water. Stir with hands; dirt will fall to the bottom of the bowl. To prevent mushrooms from absorbing water, do not let them soak. Remove mushrooms from water, and place on a cutting board. Slice about ¼ inch thick.

Heat 1 tablespoon oil in a large skillet on medium. Sauté onion for about 15 minutes, stirring occasionally, until brown and crispy. Remove and set aside. Add 1 tablespoon of oil and 1 tablespoon butter or margarine to skillet. Increase heat to medium/medium-high. Sauté mushrooms, stirring constantly, for about 2-3 minutes, until just cooked. Remove from skillet and set aside. (Drain before serving.)

When steaks are done, sprinkle with salt and pepper. Reserve half the steaks (1 pound) for the next 2 recipes. Let steaks rest 5 minutes before cutting. Cut steak off of bone, slice ¼-inch strips, and transfer to serving platter. Top with onions and mushrooms and pass at the table family style. Good served with twice-baked potatoes and mixed green salad. Yield: 4 servings

BEFORE SERVING

Reserve half (1 pound) steaks from Steak Supreme for:
- Steak and Tomato Salad
- Steak Fajitas

Steak and Tomato Salad

1 cup penne pasta or macaroni
1 head Romaine lettuce
2 ribs celery
½ cup grape tomatoes
½ cup petite baby carrots
1 cup cubed Cheddar cheese
Half of reserved steak from Steak Supreme (see page 104)
Bottled red wine vinaigrette salad dressing

Cook pasta according to package directions; drain and cool. Meanwhile, place lettuce on a large cutting board. Using a serrated knife, cut into 1-inch strips. Gather lettuce into a large bowl and cover with cold water. Use your hand to stir the lettuce so dirt can fall to the bottom. Gather the lettuce, carrying it up out of the water and into a salad spinner, rotating to dry (or pat dry with towels).

Rinse and trim leaves and ends of celery; cut in half crosswise. Cut lengthwise into sticks, then crosswise to dice. Rinse tomatoes. Cut in half. Slice steak into ¼-inch strips. Cut strips in half. Toss pasta, lettuce, celery, tomatoes, carrots, cheese, steak, and salad dressing in a large salad bowl. Divide salad onto 4 plates. Good served with multigrain crackers. Yield: 4 servings

Steak Fajitas

1 onion
1 green pepper
1 clove garlic
2 tablespoons oil
Half reserved steak from Steak Supreme (see page 104)
½ teaspoon chili powder
¼ teaspoon cumin
¼ teaspoon cayenne pepper
1 lime
Salt and pepper to taste
1 (8-count) package flour tortillas
1 cup grated Cheddar cheese
Bottled salsa
Sour cream

Use a chef's knife to cut onion in half on a cutting board. Peel off outer skin; cut out the root end. Cut onion into thin slices. Rinse and cut green pepper in half. Pull out and discard seeds. Slice into strips. Using the flat side of a chef's knife, press down on the clove of garlic to break the skin. Peel off skin. Trim off root end. Score; then cut to mince. Heat oil in a large skillet on medium. Add onion and sauté 5 minutes; then add pepper and sauté 2 additional minutes until crisp-tender. Add garlic and sauté a minute longer.

Meanwhile, cut steak into slices about ¼ inch thick. Add steak to vegetables in skillet. Add chili powder, cumin, and cayenne pepper. Cut lime in half and squeeze juice into a small bowl. Stick a fork in the lime half and rub fork back and forth to squeeze as much juice as possible. Remove seeds and pour lime over the steak and vegetables. Add salt and pepper to taste.

Warm tortillas according to package directions or layer tortillas between damp paper towels and warm in microwave oven for about 30 - 45 seconds. Divide steak and vegetables between tortillas. Top with cheese, salsa, and sour cream. Good served with tortilla chips and guacamole. Yield: 8 fajitas

Three-Day Plan

Day 1: Asian Pepper Steak ⟶ **Day 2:** Spicy Steak & Eggs ⟶
Day 3: Philly Cheese Steak Sandwiches

Asian Pepper Steak

3 tablespoons soy sauce
7 tablespoons oil, divided
1 tablespoon sake or white wine
¼ teaspoon sugar
¼ teaspoon salt
¼ teaspoon garlic powder
¼ teaspoon black pepper
2 pounds of sirloin steak
1 tablespoon cornstarch
1 green pepper
2 onions
2 tomatoes
Salt to taste

Mix ingredients for marinade in a large bowl: soy sauce, 1 tablespoon oil, sake or wine, sugar, salt, garlic powder, and pepper. Steak is easier to slice if it's slightly frozen. Use a cutting board to cut steak lengthwise into 2-inch wide strips, then crosswise into ¼-inch strips. Place in marinade while preparing other ingredients.

Cut onion in half. Peel off outer skin. Cut onion into wedges connected by the root end. Rinse and cut green pepper in half. Pull out and discard seeds. Slice into strips; then cut each strip in half crosswise. Remove the core and trim ends of tomatoes. Cut each into 8 wedges.

Heat 3 tablespoons oil in large skillet or wok over medium-high heat. Drain meat and reserve marinade. Add cornstarch to the marinade and stir to combine; set aside. Fry meat quickly until browned. Remove from skillet and set aside. Reserve half of the meat for the next 2 recipes.

Add 3 tablespoons oil. Add onion and stir-fry for 5 minutes. Add pepper to onion and continue to stir-fry 5 additional minutes. Pour marinade on one side of the skillet or wok and stir. The sauce should thicken quickly. Add tomatoes and meat at the very end. Taste, adding salt if needed. Good served over rice. Yield: 4 servings

BEFORE SERVING

Reserve half of steak from Asian Pepper Steak for:
- Spicy Steak & Eggs
- Philly Cheese Steak Sandwiches

Spicy Steak & Eggs

2 tablespoons butter or margarine
Half of reserved Asian Pepper Steak (see previous page)
8 eggs
4 slices American cheese
1 teaspoon hot pepper sauce
Salt and pepper
1 orange

Melt butter or margarine in a large non-stick skillet over low heat. Sauté steak for a minute, just until warm. Remove from pan and keep warm in a covered casserole dish in the oven set to 200 degrees F. Cut orange with peel into ¼-inch slices and set aside.

Crack eggs into a large bowl. Beat eggs with a wire whisk until combined. Tear American cheese slices into bowl with eggs. Add hot pepper sauce. Pour egg/cheese mixture into skillet. Cook, stirring constantly, until cheese is melted and eggs are scrambled. Sprinkle with salt and pepper. Serve eggs with steak and garnish with an orange slice. Good served with whole-wheat toast and hash-brown potatoes. Yield: 4 servings

Philly Cheese Steak Sandwiches

1 onion
1 green pepper
1 clove garlic
½ of reserved Asian Pepper Steak (see page 108)
4 slices Provolone cheese
4 submarine sandwich rolls
About 2 tablespoons butter or margarine

Use a chef's knife to cut onion in half on a cutting board. Peel off outer skin; cut out the root end. Cut onion into thin slices. Rinse and cut green pepper in half. Pull out and discard seeds. Slice into strips. Using the flat side of a chef's knife, press down on the clove of garlic to break the skin. Peel off skin. Trim off root end. Score; then cut to mince.

Heat oil in a large skillet on medium. Add onion and pepper. Sauté 5 - 10 minutes until crisp-tender. Add garlic and sauté a minute longer. Add steak slices and heat just until warm. Meanwhile, toast rolls and spread with butter or margarine. Pile steak, vegetables, and cheese on rolls. Broil 1 - 2 minutes to melt cheese. Serve immediately. Good served with breaded eggplant. Yield: 4 servings

My Family Favorite Beef Steak Three-Day Plan

Day 1: _____ ↗ **Day 2:** _____

↗ **Day 3:** _____

Where to find these recipes: _____

_____

_____

(Cookbook title with page #, recipe box, website, etc.)

BEFORE SERVING

Reserve _____ for:

- ♦ _____
- ♦ _____

Chapter 9: Beef Roasts

Beef roasts are easy to make. Sprinkle with herbs and cook in the oven or on the stove until done. Some roasts, such as prime rib, are tender and can be roasted, uncovered, in the oven. Some roasts, such as brisket, chuck, or arm, are less tender and need to be cooked with liquid. These roasts are called "pot roasts" because they are cooked in a pot on the stove with water, ketchup, wine, or other liquids for several hours. To keep in the juices from any type of roast, allow it to rest for 10 minutes before carving. For tender meat, always cut across the grain.

Three-Day Plan

Day 1: Easy French Dip Sandwiches ⟶ **Day 2:** Beef-Vegetable Soup ⟶ **Day 3:** Homemade Beef Pot Pie

Easy French Dip Sandwiches

1 (2 - 2½-pound) boneless chuck roast
2 cups beef broth
OR 2 cups water and 2 teaspoons beef soup base
2 tablespoons soy sauce
½ teaspoon rosemary
½ teaspoon thyme
½ teaspoon garlic
1 tablespoon chopped fresh parsley
OR 1 teaspoon dried parsley
4 - 8 hard rolls

Place roast in slow cooker. Add beef broth or water and soup base, soy sauce, rosemary, thyme, and garlic. Cover and cook on high (so the broth simmers) for 4 hours. Trim and discard fat from beef. Remove beef from broth and place in a casserole dish. Cover and keep broth warm. Shred beef by pulling apart with 2 forks.

For fresh parsley, place a small bunch in a colander and rinse under cold water. Rub the parsley with your fingers to remove dirt. Shake off excess water. Pat dry with a paper towel. Hold the parsley in a bunch and cut the leaves from the stems. Discard stems. Place leaves in a bowl and snip with kitchen shears or use a knife to chop on a cutting board. Sprinkle beef with parsley.

Before serving, reserve half of the roast for the next two meals. Toast rolls. Use tongs to place shredded beef on rolls. Ladle broth for dipping into custard cups, one per person, and place on each plate. To eat, dip sandwich into broth. Good served with sweet potato fries and broccoli salad. After serving, store beef and broth separately. Keep the remaining broth for tomorrow's dinner. Good served with sweet potato fries. Yield: 4 servings

BEFORE SERVING:

Reserve half of the beef from Easy French Dip Sandwiches for:
- Beef-Vegetable Soup
- Homemade Beef Pot Pie

AFTER SERVING:

Reserve the broth from Easy French Dip Sandwiches for:
- Beef-Vegetable Soup

Beef-Vegetable Soup

1 onion
1 tablespoon oil
3 carrots
3 stalks celery
4 medium-sized red potatoes
4 cups beef broth
OR 4 cups water and 4 teaspoons beef soup base
Reserved broth from Easy French Dip Sandwiches (see page 112)
Water
1 (8-oz.) can tomato sauce
1 cup frozen peas
Reserved roast from Easy French Dip Sandwiches (see page 112)
1 tablespoon corn starch
¼ cup water
Salt and pepper to taste

Use a chef's knife to cut onion in half on a cutting board. Peel off outer skin; cut out the root end. Score and chop. Pare, rinse, and trim ends of carrots. To prevent carrot from rolling, cut a flat edge, lengthwise. Cut lengthwise into slices. Then cut slices lengthwise into sticks; cut crosswise to dice. Rinse and trim leaves and ends of celery. Cut crosswise in half. Cut lengthwise into sticks and crosswise to dice.

Heat oil in a large (4-quart) pot on medium. Sauté onion, carrot, and celery for 5 - 10 minutes. Meanwhile, pare and rinse potatoes. Slice and dice; set aside. Add 4 cups broth or water and soup base to pot.

> Easy variation:
> Replace carrots, celery, and peas for 2 (16-oz.) packages frozen mixed vegetables or 2 (15-oz.) cans mixed vegetables. Add frozen vegetables with potatoes, or add canned vegetables with beef. Reduce cooking time from 45 minutes to 20 minutes.

Add enough water to reserved broth from French Dip Sandwiches to make 1½ cups. Add to pot, along with tomato sauce and potatoes. Bring to boil over high heat; then turn down heat to very low, cover, and simmer for 45 minutes.

To make bite-sized pieces, cut across long strands of shredded beef. Add beef and peas to soup and increase heat to return to boil. Use a fork to mix cornstarch with ¼ cup water. Add to soup while stirring until thickened. Turn down heat to low and simmer 5 minutes more. Taste and add salt and pepper if needed. When serving, keep in mind you will need about half the soup for the next meal, Beef Pot Pie. Beef-Vegetable Soup is good served with rye crackers and Swiss cheese. Yield: 4 servings

Homemade Beef Pot Pie

Dough for 2-crust pie:
2 cups flour
½ teaspoon salt
⅔ cup shortening, butter, or margarine
6 tablespoons cold water, approximately

Easy variation: Purchase prepared pie dough.

For Filling:
Reserved Beef-Vegetable Soup (see previous page)
1 tablespoon flour

For pie dough, measure and mix flour and salt in a medium-sized bowl. Cut in shortening, butter, or margarine with a pastry blender or 2 knives until it resembles meal. Stir in ¼ cup water with a fork. Add additional water, 1 tablespoon at a time, just until dough is mixed and pulls away from the sides of the bowl. Let dough rest 15 minutes in freezer or 1 hour in refrigerator.

Preheat oven to 425 degrees F. Divide dough in two. Roll out one portion of dough by rolling from the center outward into a 12-inch circle about ¼ inch thick. Place in a 9-inch pie plate (deep dish if you have one) for bottom crust. For filling, mix 1 tablespoon flour into reserved soup. Pour filling into pastry-lined pie plate. Roll out remaining dough into an 11-inch circle about ¼ inch thick for top crust.

Fold top crust in half; then fold in half again to make a triangle with a curved edge. Use a butter knife to make 4 small slits, 2 on each fold, to allow steam to escape. Place triangle of dough on filling with the point in the center, and unfold top crust, revealing slits. Fold any excess dough from the top crust under the edge of the bottom crust. Crimp edges with floured fingers. To crimp, pinch dough with thumb and pointer finger of left hand and press pointer finger from right hand into pinched dough to form a raised edge. Repeat all the way around the rim of the pie.

Cover edge of pie crust with pie shield or strip of aluminum foil. Bake at 425 degrees F. for 10 minutes; then turn heat down to 375 degrees F. for 30 - 40 minutes or until light brown, removing pie shield for the last 15 minutes of baking to brown crust. Good served with a mixed green salad. Filling is very hot, so use caution. Yield: 1 pie; 4 - 6 servings

Three-Day Plan

Day 1: Nana's Beef Brisket ⟶ **Day 2:** BBQ Beef Sandwiches ⟶ **Day 3:** Borscht

Nana's Beef Brisket

1 tablespoon vegetable oil
1 (2 - 3-pound) beef brisket
1 onion
¼ cup ketchup
4 red potatoes
4 ribs celery
4 large carrots

Heat oil in large (4 - 6-quart) pot over medium to medium-high heat. Sear brisket to seal in juices by frying until brown, about 5 minutes on each side. Transfer to slow cooker OR keep in pot to simmer on stove. Meanwhile, cut onion in half on a cutting board using a chef's knife. Peel off outer skin; cut out the root end. Cut onion into thick slices and add onion to pot. Pour and spread ketchup on top of brisket. For slow cooker: cover and heat for 5 - 6 hours on high. For stovetop: cover and turn down heat to very low and simmer for 3 hours. For either method, check brisket before the last hour of cooking time, and add broth or water to keep brisket from drying out.

Remove brisket from pot. Let rest while preparing vegetables. Pare, rinse, and cut potatoes into quarters. Rinse and trim leaves and ends of celery; cut into approximately 2-inch lengths. Pare, rinse, and trim ends of carrots. Cut in half, lengthwise. Place flat side down and cut into approximately 1-inch lengths.

Add potatoes, celery, and carrots to pot. Carve brisket across the grain into ¼-inch slices; place on top of vegetables. Cover and simmer on low for an additional 2 hours on high in slow cooker OR bring to a boil, turn down to low and simmer an additional 1 hour on stovetop.

Before serving, reserve half of brisket for the next two dinners. To serve, spoon au jus (broth) over meat and vegetables. Good served with sweet and sour red cabbage and multigrain rolls. Yield: 4 servings

BEFORE SERVING

Reserve half of the meat from Nana's Beef Brisket for:
- BBQ Beef Sandwiches
- Borscht

BBQ Beef Sandwiches

1 onion
1 tablespoon oil
1 cup ketchup
2 tablespoons cider vinegar
1 tablespoon Worcestershire sauce
1 teaspoon sugar
Half of the reserved beef from Nana's Beef Brisket (see previous page)
Salt and pepper to taste
4 hamburger buns

Using a chef's knife, cut onion in half lengthwise on a cutting board. Peel off outer skin; cut out the root end. Place onion flat side down. Score; then cut to dice. Heat oil in a large skillet on medium. Sauté onion for about 10 minutes or until soft and lightly browned. Add ketchup, vinegar, Worcestershire sauce, and sugar.

Increase heat to medium-high while stirring, just until the mixture comes to a boil. Add beef and return to a boil. Turn down heat to low. Simmer for about 5 minutes or until heated through, stirring occasionally. Add salt and pepper to taste. Serve on toasted buns. Good served with au gratin potatoes and baked beans. Yield: 4 servings.

Borscht

1 onion
2 carrots
About ¼ small head of cabbage
OR 2 cups shredded cabbage
3 cups beef broth
OR 3 cups water and 3 teaspoons beef soup base
1 cup water
1 (15-oz.) can sliced beets
Half of reserved beef from Nana's Beef Brisket (see page 117)
1 tablespoon lemon juice
1 (12-oz.) carton sour cream

Trim ends of onion, keeping onion whole. Peel off outer skin. Grate onion into a bowl. Pare, rinse, and trim ends of carrots; cut in half crosswise. To prevent carrot from rolling, cut a flat edge, lengthwise. Cut lengthwise into slices. Then cut slices lengthwise into sticks. Peel off and discard outer leaves of cabbage. Rinse under cold water. Cut in half lengthwise through the core. Cut each cabbage half through the core to make fourths. If there are bugs or dirt, soak cabbage in a bowl of salted water to cover for 15 minutes. Then place flat edge of cabbage on a cutting board. Cut out and discard core, and slice into ⅛-inch strips.

Pour beef broth (or water and soup base) and 1 cup water into a large pot; add onion and carrots. Bring to a boil on high heat; then turn down to low and cover. Simmer 20 minutes. Add cabbage and simmer an additional 10 minutes, uncovered. Meanwhile, cut sliced beets and beef brisket into sticks. Add to pot and simmer an additional 2 minutes. Add lemon juice and serve hot in soup mugs or bowls with a dollop of sour cream. Good served with pumpernickel bread. Yield: 4 servings

Three-Day Plan

Day 1: Corned Beef & Cabbage ⟶ **Day 2:** Reuben Sandwiches ⟶ **Day 3:** Corned Beef Hash

Corned Beef & Cabbage

2 - 3-pound corned beef brisket
8 medium-sized, red potatoes
1 head cabbage

Rinse corned beef with cold water to remove excess spices and salt; place in a large (4 - 6-quart) pot. Cover with water. Bring to a boil over high heat. Turn down heat to very low. Simmer, covered, until tender, about 3 hours.

Remove beef from pot and place on a platter. Let rest 15 minutes. Meanwhile, prepare vegetables. Pare and rinse potatoes; cut into fourths. Rinse cabbage and cut in half. Then cut the cabbage into wedges, leaving cabbage leaves connected to core. Place potatoes in same pot used to cook corned beef. Bring to a boil; then turn down heat to low. Simmer, covered, for about 15 minutes. Add cabbage wedges and cook an additional 10 - 15 minutes, uncovered, or until vegetables are tender.

While vegetables are cooking, carve the corned beef cutting across the grain into thin slices on a cutting board. Keep half of corned beef warm. Reserve half of the corned beef for the next two dinners, 4 of the potatoes, and 1 cup broth for the second dinner, Corned Beef Hash. Good served with Irish Soda Bread. Yield: 4 servings

BEFORE SERVING

Reserve half of corned beef, 4 potatoes, and 1 cup broth from Corned Beef & Cabbage for:
- Reuben Sandwiches
- Corned Beef Hash

Reuben Sandwiches

8 slices rye bread
Approximately 3 tablespoons soft butter or margarine
4 - 8 slices reserved corned beef, depending on size (see previous page)
4 slices Swiss cheese
Approximately ½ cup sauerkraut

Heat a large skillet or griddle on medium. Meanwhile, assemble sandwiches. Spread butter or margarine on one side of each slice of bread. Place buttered side of bread down on plate. Place corned beef, 1 slice of cheese, and a thin layer of sauerkraut on a slice of bread. Top with a slice of bread, buttered side out, to complete the sandwich. Repeat to make 4 sandwiches.

Place sandwiches in a dry skillet (no oil needed) because the butter or margarine will keep the bread from sticking to the skillet. Cook just a few minutes, until lightly browned; then carefully turn over, keeping the sandwich filling intact. Fry second side until lightly browned. Serve warm. Good served with navy bean soup and dill pickles. Yield: 4 sandwiches

Corned Beef Hash

2 tablespoon oil
1 onion
2 tablespoons chopped fresh parsley
OR 2 teaspoons dried parsley
Half of the reserved Corned Beef (see page 120)
4 cooked potatoes reserved from Corned Beef & Cabbage (see page 120)
About 1 cup broth from cooking Corned Beef (see page 120)
Salt and pepper to taste

Heat oil in large skillet on low. Using a chef's knife, cut onion in half lengthwise on a cutting board. Peel off outer skin; cut out the root end. Place onion flat side down. Score; then cut to dice. Add onion to skillet; sauté for 5 minutes.

> Variation:
> Red Flannel Hash: add 1 cup cooked diced beets to skillet when adding other ingredients.

For fresh parsley, place a small bunch in a colander and rinse under cold water. Rub the parsley with your fingers to remove dirt. Shake off excess water. Pat dry with a paper towel. Hold the parsley in a bunch and cut the leaves from the stems. Discard stems. Place leaves in a bowl and snip with kitchen shears or use a knife to chop on a cutting board. Set aside.

Cut corned beef and potatoes into bite-sized pieces; add to skillet along with parsley and half of broth. Turn up heat to medium and fry until brown, about 10 minutes. Turn over and fry until brown. Add more broth if needed. Add salt and pepper to taste. Good served with fried or poached eggs and biscuits. Yield: 4 servings

My Family Favorite Beef Roast Three-Day Plan

Day 1: _____ ⤳ **Day 2:** _____

⤳ **Day 3:** _____

Where to find these recipes: ─────────────────────

────────────────────────────────────

────────────────────────────────────

(*Cookbook title with page #, recipe box, website, etc.*)

BEFORE SERVING

Reserve _____ for:

♦ _____

♦ _____

Delicious Dinners with Pork

Variety

Pork is used for spicy, salty, smoky sausage, bacon, ham, and a variety of roasts, ribs, and chops. Pork is used in every meal: breakfast, lunch, and dinner. Our family enjoys eating typical dishes served at breakfast for dinner—see the recipes included for casseroles, sandwiches, and wraps.

Health

Consider purchasing healthier options for pork, from low-salt bacon to natural ham and leaner pork. Even though pork is advertised as "the other white meat," like beef and lamb, it is considered red meat, which is high in cholesterol.

Defrost

Like other meats, the safest way to defrost pork is in the refrigerator. If you defrost it in the microwave, cook it right after defrosting. Cook ground pork thoroughly until meat is no longer pink. Cook chops and roasts to at least 145 degrees F. and ground pork mixtures such as meatloaf to 160 degrees F.

To see more information about pork, see the U.S. Department of Agriculture link:
http://www.fsis.usda.gov/factsheets/Pork_From_Farm_to_Table/index.asp

Chapter 10: Pork Sausage

Three-Day Plan

Day 1: Breakfast-for-Dinner Casserole ⟶ **Day 2:** Sausage-Mushroom Pizza ⟶ **Day 3:** Biscuits & Sausage Gravy

Breakfast-for-Dinner Casserole

Sausage:
2 pounds ground pork
¼ pound ground pork fat (optional)
2 teaspoons sage
2 teaspoons paprika
1 teaspoon thyme
2 teaspoons salt
1 teaspoon black pepper

Easy variation: Substitute 2 pounds prepared bulk sausage for homemade sausage mixture.

Egg mixture:
1 cup seasoned croutons
1 cup cubed Monterey Jack cheese
8 eggs
¼ cup milk

Measure and mix ground pork, pork fat, sage, paprika, thyme, salt, and pepper in a large bowl. Brown in a skillet over medium heat, separating meat into chunks with a fork or pancake turner. Cook until no longer pink and cooked through. Reserve about two-thirds of sausage (about 1⅓ pounds) for the next two meals.

Preheat oven to 350 degrees F. Grease an 8x8x2-inch glass baking dish. Distribute croutons, sausage, and cheese evenly in baking dish. Beat eggs in a large bowl; add milk. Pour egg mixture over sausage mixture. Bake for 30 - 35 minutes or until top is lightly browned and eggs are set. Good served with twice baked potatoes and pear and walnut salad. Yield: 4 servings

Spicy variation: Add ½ teaspoon red pepper flakes to sausage mixture before cooking.

> ### BEFORE SERVING
> Reserve two-thirds (1⅓ pounds) of cooked sausage from Breakfast-for-Dinner Casserole for:
> - Sausage-Mushroom Pizza
> - Biscuits & Sausage Gravy

Sausage-Mushroom Pizza

Dough:
¾ cup water
¾ teaspoon salt
1 tablespoon oil
2 cups bread flour
1 teaspoon active-dry yeast

Easy variation: Substitute premade pizza crust for the dough.

Pizza:
1 tablespoon cornmeal
½ cup tomato sauce
¼ teaspoon oregano
1½ cups grated mozzarella cheese
2 tablespoons Parmesan cheese
Half of reserved sausage from Breakfast-for-Dinner Casserole (see previous page)
6 oz. (about 8 medium) button mushrooms

For bread machine, add ingredients to bread machine in order: water, salt, oil, bread flour, whole-wheat flour, and yeast. Follow manufacturer's directions for mixing "dough," which should mix the dough and let it rise, but not bake.

To mix by hand, the ingredients are not listed in the order in which you add them. Measure water in a glass measuring cup and warm in microwave for about 30 seconds. Test the temperature by dipping your finger in the water and dripping it on your wrist. It should feel warm but not hot. If the water is too hot, it will kill the yeast, but if it's not hot enough, the bread will not rise. Pour water into a large bowl. Add the yeast; stir with a wooden spoon until it is dissolved. Add salt, oil, and bread flour. Stir to combine. Place dough on a floured cloth or board. Knead for 5 - 8 minutes by folding and pressing dough with the heel of your hand. Give a quarter turn, fold and press. The dough should be smooth and elastic after kneading. Place the dough back in the mixing bowl, cover with a dishtowel, and let rise 1 - 1½ hours until doubled in bulk.

When dough is nearly done rising, prepare mushrooms. Place mushrooms in a bowl of cold water. Stir with hands; dirt will fall to the bottom of the bowl. To prevent mushrooms from absorbing water, do not let soak. Remove mushrooms from water, and place on a cutting board. Pat dry. Slice about ¼ inch thick. Heat 1 tablespoon oil in a large skillet on medium/medium-high. Sauté mushrooms, stirring constantly, for about 3 minutes, until just brown and slightly smaller in size. Remove from skillet to a bowl and set aside. (Drain before placing on pizza.)

Move the oven rack to the lowest position. Preheat the oven to 450 degrees F. Sprinkle cornmeal on a large (12-inch) ungreased pizza stone or greased large cookie sheet. Place dough on pizza stone or cookie sheet. Gently press, stretch, and pull pizza dough with floured hands to make a 12-inch circle, building up dough slightly to form an edge. Prick the dough with a fork so it won't bubble up when baked. Bake crust for 10 minutes. Spread sauce to edge of crust. Top with oregano, cheeses, sausage, and drained mushrooms. Bake approximately 10 minutes or until cheese is melted and lightly browned. Good served with a mixed green salad. Yield: 1 (12-inch) pizza

Biscuits & Sausage Gravy

Biscuits:
2 cups flour
1 tablespoon baking powder
1 teaspoon salt
¼ cup shortening
¾ cup milk

Sausage Gravy:
Half of reserved sausage from Breakfast-for-Dinner Casserole (see page 125)
3 tablespoons butter or margarine
4 tablespoons flour
2 cups milk (or half water)
Salt and pepper to taste

Preheat oven to 450 degrees F. Measure flour, baking powder, and salt into a large bowl. Cut in shortening with a pastry blender or two butter knives until it resembles meal. Use a fork to stir in the milk. Gather dough and place on floured cloth or board.
Knead dough by folding, pressing with palms, and turning a quarter turn; repeat 20 times. Use a rolling pin to roll ½ inch thick. Cut into 2-inch rounds with floured biscuit cutter or drinking glass. Place on ungreased baking sheet. Bake about 10 minutes, or until golden brown. Yield: 1 dozen biscuits

Easy variation: Substitute 1 can refrigerated biscuit dough for homemade biscuits. Bake according to package directions.

While biscuits are baking, melt butter or margarine in a large skillet and heat on medium. Add flour, stirring until combined and bubbly. Whisk in milk, stirring until thickened. Stir in reserved sausage with a wooden spoon. Serve over split, hot biscuits. Good served with fresh fruit salad. Yield: 4 servings

Three-Day Plan

Day 1: Busy Day Goulash ⟶ **Day 2:** Hot Dog Bean Bake ⟶ **Day 3:** Mac 'n Cheese with Hot Dogs

Busy Day Goulash

¼ cup butter or margarine
2 onions
2 green peppers
1 (15-oz.) can diced tomatoes
¼ teaspoon paprika
1 (10-count) package hot dogs
Salt and pepper to taste
1 (12-oz.) package wide egg noodles

Using a chef's knife, cut onion in half on a cutting board. Peel off outer skin; cut out the root end. Cut onion into thin slices. Rinse and cut green peppers in half. Pull out and discard seeds. Slice into strips. Melt butter or margarine in large skillet over medium-low heat. Add onions and peppers. Sauté until onions are transparent, about 10 minutes, stirring occasionally.

Add tomatoes with juice and paprika. Bring to a boil over medium-high heat. Turn down to low, cover, and simmer 15 minutes. Meanwhile, cook noodles according to package directions; drain. Cut 4 hot dogs in half lengthwise, then crosswise into ½-inch pieces. Add to skillet and cook until heated through. Reserve remaining 6 hot dogs for the next two dinners. Add salt and pepper to taste. Serve goulash over noodles. Good served with braised cabbage. Yield: 4 servings

BEFORE SERVING
Reserve 6 hot dogs for:
- Hot Dog Bean Bake
- Mac 'n Cheese with Hot Dogs

Hot Dog Bean Bake

1 (16-oz.) can baked beans
1 (15-oz.) can kidney beans
1 (15-oz.) can baby lima beans
1 onion
3 hot dogs reserved from Busy Day Goulash (see previous page)
½ cup ketchup
½ cup water
1 teaspoon vinegar
1 teaspoon soy sauce
½ cup brown sugar
½ teaspoon dry mustard
2 slices bacon

Preheat oven to 300 degrees F. Grease a 2-quart casserole dish. Use a colander to drain and rinse baked beans, kidney beans, and lima beans. Pour into prepared casserole dish. Using a chef's knife, cut onion in half lengthwise on a cutting board. Peel off outer skin; cut out the root end. Place onion flat side down. Score; then cut to dice. Add to beans.

Cut hot dogs in half lengthwise, then crosswise into ½-inch pieces. Add hot dogs, ketchup, water, vinegar, soy sauce, brown sugar, and mustard; stir to combine. Top with bacon. Bake uncovered for 1 hour or until beans are bubbly. Good served with Boston Brown Bread and a mixed green salad. Yield: 4 servings

Mac 'n Cheese with Hot Dogs

1 (12-oz.) package whole grain mostaccioli or ziti
4 tablespoons butter or margarine, divided
4 tablespoons flour
2 cups milk
2 cups grated Cheddar cheese
3 hot dogs reserved from Busy Day Goulash (see page 129)
¼ cup whole-wheat bread crumbs

Preheat oven to 350 degrees F. Grease a 2-quart casserole dish. Cook mostaccioli or ziti according to package directions; drain.

Meanwhile, melt 3 tablespoons butter or margarine in a medium-sized (3-quart) saucepan over medium heat. Add flour; cook and stir 1 minute. Whisk in milk and cook until thickened, stirring frequently. Add cheese, stirring with a wooden spoon until melted. Stir in cooked mostaccioli or ziti.

Cut hot dogs in half lengthwise, then crosswise into ½-inch pieces. Add hot dogs to cheese-pasta mixture. Pour hot dog mixture into prepared casserole dish. Sprinkle on breadcrumbs and dot with remaining butter or margarine. Bake until hot and bubbly, about 20 minutes. Good served with broccoli salad. Yield: 4 servings

> Easy variation: Substitute a family-size box of macaroni and cheese for the homemade recipe. Prepare according to package directions. Then mix with hot dogs and bake as above.

Three-Day Plan

Day 1: Brats on Buns ⟶ **Day 2:** Lentil Soup with Brats ⟶ **Day 3:** Sausage Stew

Brats on Buns

8 smoked Bratwurst
4 Bratwurst buns (large hot dog buns)
Toppings:
- Mustard
- Ketchup
- Sauerkraut
- Chopped sweet or dill pickle
- Sweet or hot peppers
- Shredded Cheddar cheese
- Chopped onion

To cook outdoors: fire up coals or heat gas grill. Grill Bratwurst 8-10 minutes over medium-low flame turning frequently to brown evenly.

To cook indoors: Heat ⅔ cup water in a large skillet to boiling. Add Bratwurst, cover, and turn heat to low. Cook 5 minutes; turn Bratwurst over. Cover and cook 5 minutes more. Remove cover and drain water. Cook an additional 4 minutes to brown Brats lightly.

Reserve 4 Brats for the next 2 dinners. Toast buns and serve with favorite toppings: mustard, ketchup, sauerkraut, pickle, peppers, onions, and/or cheese. Good served with German potato salad and applesauce.

Note: When serving Bratwurst to children, prevent choking by cutting the Bratwurst in half, lengthwise, before serving.

BEFORE SERVING
Reserve 4 Bratwurst from Brats on Buns for:
- Lentil Soup with Brats
- Sausage Stew

Lentil Soup with Brats

1½ cups dried lentils
2 Bratwurst reserved from Brats on Buns (see previous page)
2 large onions
2 ribs celery
3 medium potatoes
1 quart water
1 quart chicken broth
OR 1 quart water and 4 teaspoons chicken soup base
3 tablespoons flour
Salt and pepper to taste

Pick through lentils, discarding dirt and rocks. Rinse and cover in cold water; soak for two hours.

Using a chef's knife, cut onions in half lengthwise on a cutting board. Peel off outer skin; cut out the root end. Place onion flat side down. Score; then cut to dice. Rinse and trim leaves and ends of celery; cut in half crosswise. Cut lengthwise into sticks, then crosswise to dice. Pare and rinse potatoes. Using a cutting board, cut into ½-inch slices. Cut slices into ½-inch sticks; then cut crosswise to dice. Cut Bratwurst in half, lengthwise, then crosswise into ½-inch pieces. Drain lentils.

Combine onion, celery, potatoes, 1 quart water, chicken broth (or water and soup base), and lentils in a large (4 - 6) pot. Bring to a boil. Turn down heat to low. Cover and simmer 30 - 60 minutes or until lentils and vegetables are soft. Meanwhile, brown flour in a small skillet over low heat, stirring constantly so flour does not burn. Whisk into soup, stirring in quickly so lumps won't form. Add Bratwurst. Continue to simmer, uncovered, for five minutes. Season to taste with salt and pepper. Good served with pumpernickel bread. Yield: 4-6 servings

Sausage Stew

2 tablespoons butter or margarine
1 onion
1 green pepper
1 clove garlic
1 (14½-oz.) can diced tomatoes
¼ cup chopped fresh parsley
OR 4 teaspoons dried parsley
2 bay leaves
¼ teaspoon thyme
⅛ teaspoon sugar
2 teaspoons cornstarch
¼ cup water
½ teaspoon hot pepper sauce
2 Bratwurst reserved from Brats on Buns (see page 132)

Using a chef's knife, cut onion in half lengthwise on a cutting board. Peel off outer skin; cut out the root end. Place onion flat side down. Score; then cut to dice. Rinse and cut green pepper in half. Pull out and discard seeds. Slice into strips; then cut across strips to dice. Press the flat side of a chef's knife on garlic clove to break skin. Peel off skin. Trim off root end. Score; then cut to mince.

For fresh parsley, place a big bunch in a colander and rinse under cold water. Rub the parsley with your fingers to remove dirt. Shake off excess water. Pat dry with a paper towel. Hold the parsley in a bunch and cut the leaves from the stems. Discard stems. Place leaves in a bowl and snip with kitchen shears or use a knife to chop on a cutting board. Set aside.

Melt butter or margarine in a large skillet over medium heat. Sauté onion and pepper until soft, 5 - 10 minutes. Add garlic to skillet and sauté 1 minute more. Add tomatoes with juice, parsley, bay leaves, thyme, salt, and sugar; stir to combine. Bring to a boil; then turn down to low, cover, and simmer 15 minutes. Measure cornstarch, water, and pepper sauce in a small bowl and stir with a fork. Add to skillet, stirring until mixture thickens slightly. Remove bay leaves and discard. Cut Bratwurst in half, lengthwise, then crosswise into half circles. Add to stew. Good served over brown and wild rice pilaf. Yield: 4 servings

My Family Favorite Sausage Three-Day Plan

Day 1: _____ ↪ **Day 2:** _____

↪ **Day 3:** _____

Where to find these recipes: ─────────────────

─────────────────────────────

─────────────────────────────

(*Cookbook title with page #, recipe box, website, etc.*)

BEFORE SERVING

Reserve _____ for:

- ♦ _____
- ♦ _____

Chapter 11: Pork Chops

I like to buy boneless pork chops because they cook quickly. Bones add flavor, but they take longer to cook. Center-cut pork chops (with a T-shaped bone) are tender and flavorful. You can buy either kind for Favorite Pork Chops, but keep in mind that you will need to cook chops with bones about twice as long.

Pork works well paired with other flavors like soy sauce and balsamic vinegar, or spicy red peppers. Cook pork chops to an internal temperature of 145 degrees F. After checking the temperature, allow the meat to rest for 3 minutes.

See this link from the U.S. Department of Agriculture (USDA) for an article explaining the recently revised cooking temperature from 160 to 145 degrees for pork chops:
http://www.fsis.usda.gov/News_&_Events/NR_052411_01/index.asp

Three-Day Plan
Day 1: Favorite Pork Chops ⟶ **Day 2:** Pork Fried Rice ⟶ **Day 3:** Hot & Sour Soup

Favorite Pork Chops

2 cups white or brown rice
1 teaspoon salt
4 tablespoons oil, divided
6 (4 - 6 oz. each) boneless pork chops
Salt and pepper
⅓ cup balsamic vinegar
1 tablespoon soy sauce

Heat oven to 400 degrees F. Use a large (4-quart) pot to cook rice. Measure rice and twice as much water (4 cups for white rice; 4 ½ cups for brown rice) into pot. Add salt and 2 tablespoons oil. Bring to a boil over high heat. Stir once with a fork, turn down to very low, cover, and cook for 20 minutes for white rice and 40 minutes for brown rice. Do not lift cover.

Meanwhile, heat 2 tablespoons oil in a large skillet on medium-high. Sear pork chops in two batches. Cook about 3 minutes on each side. Remove to a 9x13x2-inch glass pan. Sprinkle pork with salt and pepper. Mix vinegar and soy sauce and pour over pork. Bake for about 20 minutes or until well cooked. Let rest 3 minutes before serving. Reserve 2 pork chops for the next 2 dinners. Reserve half of the rice for tomorrow night's meal, Pork Fried Rice. Good served with sautéed spinach. Yield: 4 servings

BEFORE SERVING

Reserve 2 pork chops from Favorite Pork Chops for:
- Pork Fried Rice
- Hot & Sour Soup

Reserve 3 cups cooked rice for
- Pork Fried Rice

Pork Fried Rice

1 reserved pork chop from Favorite Pork Chops (see page 137)
½ cup frozen peas
1 carrot
1 small onion
5 green onions
½ green pepper
1 celery rib
6 tablespoons oil, divided
3 eggs
Salt and pepper to taste
3 cups cooked rice, cold, reserved from Favorite Pork Chops

Cut pork chop into thin slices; then cut slices into match sticks and set aside. Cook peas according to package directions. Meanwhile, prepare vegetables. Pare, rinse, and trim ends of carrots; cut in half crosswise. To prevent carrot from rolling, cut a flat edge, lengthwise. Cut lengthwise into slices. Then cut slices lengthwise into sticks; cut crosswise to dice. Cut onion in half lengthwise. Peel off outer skin; cut out the root end. Place onion flat side down. Score; then cut to dice. Rinse green onions. Trim top and root end, and remove loose outer skin. Cut, starting with green top, crosswise into ⅛-inch circles on a cutting board. Rinse and cut green pepper in half. (Refrigerate half to use in another meal.) Pull out and discard seeds. Slice into strips; then cut across strips to dice. Rinse and trim leaves and ends of celery; cut in half crosswise. Cut lengthwise into sticks, then crosswise to dice.

Heat 2 tablespoons oil in a large skillet or wok on medium. Beat eggs. Add to skillet and cook, stirring, just until cooked. Remove to a plate and set aside. Heat 4 tablespoons oil on medium-high. Add carrot and onion. Stir-fry for 2 minutes. Add green onions, green pepper, and celery and stir-fry for 2 minutes. Add rice and stir-fry 1 minute. Season with salt and pepper to taste. Add peas, pork, and eggs, and mix thoroughly. Good served with egg rolls. Yield: 4 servings

Hot & Sour Soup

4 dried mushrooms
2 green onions
1 (8-oz.) can bamboo shoots
¼ pound tofu
1 reserved pork chop from Favorite Pork Chops (see page 137)
1 quart chicken broth
OR 1 quart water and 4 teaspoons chicken soup base
1 tablespoon sherry
2 tablespoons wine vinegar
1 tablespoon soy sauce
2 tablespoons cornstarch
¼ cup water
½ teaspoon white pepper
1 egg
Salt

Place mushrooms in a small bowl; cover with warm water and soak for 30 minutes. Rinse green onions. Trim top and root end, and remove loose outer skin. Cut, starting with green top, diagonally in 1-inch slices and set aside. Drain mushrooms and cut off stems; squeeze dry. Cut mushrooms, bamboo shoots, tofu, and pork into thin strips.

Heat chicken broth or water and soup base in a large pot. Add mushrooms, bamboo shoots, tofu, pork, sherry, vinegar, and soy sauce. Heat to boiling over high heat. Turn down heat to medium and simmer 2 minutes. Use a fork to mix cornstarch into water in a small bowl. Stir into boiling soup. Turn heat off. Add pepper. Beat egg and slowly pour into soup while stirring. Sprinkle green onion on top. Taste soup and add salt if needed. Good topped with crispy chow mein noodles. Yield: 4 servings

My Family Favorite Pork Chop Three-Day Plan

Day 1: _____ ↗ **Day 2:** _____

↗ **Day 3:** _____

Where to find these recipes: _____

_____

_____

(*Cookbook title with page #, recipe box, website, etc.*)

BEFORE SERVING

Reserve _____ for:

- ♦ _____
- ♦ _____

Chapter 12: Pork Roasts

Like roasted beef or chicken, pork roasts are easy to make and yield several servings. Some tender pork roasts, such as loin and tenderloin, can be roasted, uncovered, in the oven. Because pork is leaner than it used to be, oven-roasted pork cooks faster and can become dried out if overcooked. Some roasts, such as pork shoulder, are less tender and need to be cooked with liquid. Whether you roast pork in the oven or simmer it in a pot, let the roast rest for 10 minutes before carving to keep in the juices.

See this U.S. Department of Agriculture (USDA) link for more about roasting pork and other meats:
http://www.fsis.usda.gov/Factsheets/Roasting_Those_Other_Holiday_Meats/index.asp

Three-Day Plan

Day 1: Pulled Pork with Honey-Mustard Sauce ⟶ **Day 2:** BBQ Pork Sandwiches ⟶ **Day 3:** Carnitas Burritos

Pulled Pork with Honey-Mustard Sauce

1 (3-pound) boneless pork shoulder roast
1 onion
1 cup ketchup
¼ cup cider vinegar
2 tablespoons packed brown sugar
1 teaspoon chili powder

Honey-Mustard Sauce:
¼ cup prepared mustard
3 tablespoons honey
3 tablespoons apple cider vinegar
2 tablespoons apple, grape, or orange juice

If your pork roast is bound with string webbing, leave it on until after cooking. Place roast in slow cooker. Trim root end of onion, but leave intact. Peel outer skin off of onion, leaving onion whole, and place in slow cooker. Mix ketchup, vinegar, brown sugar, and chili powder in a bowl. Pour over roast. Cover and cook on high (simmer) for 4 to 5 hours or until thoroughly cooked.

Remove roast from slow cooker to a plate to rest for 10 minutes. Meanwhile, prepare Honey-Mustard Sauce. Mix mustard, honey, vinegar, and fruit juice in a small saucepan and heat on low for a few minutes until warm.

Using a kitchen scissors, snip string webbing encasing roast to remove. Trim all fat from roast and discard. Cut meat into slices or shred with two forks. Place half of meat on a serving plate and reserve half for the next two dinners. Save the broth from the slow cooker in a separate container. Pour Honey-Mustard Sauce into a small pitcher such as a creamer to pass at the table. Good served with boiled new potatoes and peas. Yield: 4 servings

BEFORE SERVING

Reserve half of pork AND all of the broth in the slow cooker from Pulled Pork with Honey-Mustard Sauce for:
- BBQ Pork Sandwiches
- Carnitas Burritos

BBQ Pork Sandwiches

Half of reserved pork from Pulled Pork with Honey-Mustard Sauce (see page 143)
Reserved broth in slow cooker from Pulled Pork with Honey-Mustard Sauce (see page 143)
Barbecue sauce (see recipe following)
OR bottled barbecue sauce
4 hamburger buns

Place pork in a medium-sized saucepan. Discard fat from the surface of the reserved slow-cooker broth. Add a spoonful of reserved broth to moisten the meat. Reserve the rest of the broth for the next recipe: Carnitas Burritos. Heat on low. Either prepare barbeque sauce recipe, following, or use about a cup of bottled barbeque sauce. Pour barbeque sauce over meat, mixing gently with a fork. Heat pork and barbecue sauce, covered, on low about 5 minutes or until heated through and bubbly. Stir frequently so sauce does not burn. Serve on toasted buns. Good served with baked sweet potato fries, coleslaw, and pickles. Yield: 4 servings

BBQ Sauce

1 onion
1 tablespoon oil
1 cup ketchup
2 tablespoons cider vinegar
1 tablespoon Worcestershire sauce
1 teaspoon sugar
Salt and pepper to taste

Using a chef's knife, cut onion in half lengthwise on a cutting board. Peel off outer skin; cut out the root end. Place onion flat side down. Score; then cut to dice. Heat oil in a large skillet on medium. Sauté onion for about 10 minutes, or until soft and lightly browned. Add ketchup, vinegar, Worcestershire sauce, and sugar. Increase heat to medium-high and stir just until the mixture comes to a boil. Add salt and pepper to taste Yield: about 1¼ cups

Carnitas Burritos

Cilantro Rice:
2 tablespoons oil
1 cup white or brown rice
2 to 2¼ cups chicken broth
OR 2 to 2¼ cups water and 2 teaspoons chicken soup base
1 lime
2 tablespoons fresh cilantro

Burritos:
1 (15-oz.) can black beans
1 teaspoon cumin
1 teaspoon chili powder
¼ teaspoon cayenne pepper
Half of reserved pork from Pulled Pork with Honey-Mustard Sauce (see page 143)
Reserved broth from Pulled Pork with Honey-Mustard Sauce (see page 143)
1 (8-count) package burrito-size flour tortillas
1 cup grated Cheddar cheese
Bottled salsa
Bottled hot pepper sauce
Sour cream

First, make rice. Heat oil in a 2-quart saucepan on medium. Stir and cook rice until translucent and lightly browned, about 5 minutes. Add 2 cups broth (or water and soup base) for white rice, 2¼ cups broth (or water and soup base) for brown rice. Bring to a boil, stir once, and turn down to very low. Cover and cook undisturbed for 20 minutes for white rice, 40 minutes for brown rice, or until all water is absorbed and rice is tender. Do not lift cover.

Meanwhile, cut lime in half and squeeze juice into a small bowl. Stick a fork in the lime half and rub fork back and forth to squeeze as much juice as possible. Discard lime seeds. Swish cilantro in a bowl of cold water. Rub the leaves with your fingers to remove dirt. Shake off excess water. Pat leaves dry with a paper towel. Hold the cilantro in a bunch and cut the leaves from the stems. Discard stems. Place leaves in a bowl and snip with kitchen shears or use a knife to chop on a cutting board. Measure 2 tablespoons of cilantro. Add lime juice and cilantro to rice. Cover and turn heat off.

Drain and rinse black beans. Heat in a small saucepan over low heat. Warm reserved pork, with enough broth to moisten, in a skillet over low heat. Add cumin, chili powder, and cayenne pepper and simmer uncovered for 5 - 10 minutes or until flavors blend and meat is heated through. Add more broth if needed.

Warm tortillas according to package directions or warm in microwave between damp paper towels. Spoon meat, beans, and rice onto warm flour tortillas. Top with a spoonful each of cheese, salsa, hot sauce, and sour cream. Fold bottom edge up to keep filling in; then roll from left to right. Good served with tortilla chips and guacamole. Yield: 8 large burritos

Three-Day Plan

Day 1: Herbed Pork Loin Roast ⟶ **Day 2:** Emily's Pork Lo Mein ⟶ **Day 3:** Spicy Chili with Pork

Herbed Pork Loin Roast

2 pound pork loin roast
¼ teaspoon sage
¼ teaspoon rosemary
¼ teaspoon oregano
Pinch thyme

Place roast in an 8x8x2 or 8x10x2-inch glass baking dish. Sprinkle with sage, rosemary, oregano, and thyme. Bake at 325 degrees F. for about 90 minutes or until a meat thermometer registers 145 degrees F. Remove from oven and let rest for 10 minutes. Cut into thin slices, ⅛ - ¼ inch wide. Reserve half of the roast for the next two meals. Good served with roasted butternut squash and apple rings. Yield: 4 servings

BEFORE SERVING

Reserve half of Herbed Pork Loin Roast for:
- Emily's Pork Lo Mein
- Spicy Chili with Pork

Emily's Pork Lo Mein

1 (8-oz.) package linguine
3 tablespoons oil, divided
1 onion
1 green bell pepper
1 rib celery
1 small head broccoli
3 tablespoons water
½ teaspoon ground ginger
½ teaspoon paprika
¼ teaspoon cayenne pepper
Half of reserved Pork Loin Roast (see previous page)
1 cup chicken broth
OR 1 cup water and 1 teaspoon chicken soup base
¼ cup soy sauce
1 tablespoon molasses
2 tablespoons cider vinegar
1 tablespoon sugar
1 tablespoon cornstarch

Cook linguine according to package directions. Drain, toss with 1 tablespoon oil, and set aside. Meanwhile, prepare vegetables. Using a chef's knife, cut onion in half on a cutting board. Peel off outer skin; cut out the root end. Cut onion into thin slices. Rinse and cut green pepper in half. Pull out and discard seeds. Slice into strips. Rinse and trim leaves and ends of celery; cut in half. Cut celery crosswise into diagonal slices. Rinse and cut off broccoli florets from stem. Cut florets into bite-sized pieces of about 1 inch. Heat 2 tablespoons oil in a large skillet or wok on medium-high. Add onion, pepper, celery, and broccoli; stir-fry about 5 minutes. Add 3 tablespoons water, cover, and cook for 3 minutes or until crisp-tender. Sprinkle vegetables with ginger, paprika, and cayenne pepper.

Cut sliced pork into matchstick-size pieces; set aside. Use a fork to mix chicken broth, soy sauce, molasses, cider vinegar, sugar, and cornstarch in a bowl. Add to pan, stirring until thick and bubbly, along with pork and cooked noodles. Stir about a minute until pork and noodles are heated. Good served with crab Rangoon. Yield: 4 servings

Spicy Chili with Pork

1 onion
1 green bell pepper
Half of reserved Herbed Pork Loin Roast (see page 148)
1 tablespoon oil
2 teaspoons chili powder
1 (16-oz.) can diced tomatoes
1 (8-oz.) can tomato sauce
¼ teaspoon cayenne pepper
½ teaspoon salt
1 (15½-oz.) can kidney beans
1 cup grated Cheddar cheese
Bottled hot pepper sauce

Cut onion in half lengthwise. Peel off outer skin; cut out the root end. Place onion flat side down. Score and dice. Rinse and cut green pepper in half. Pull out and discard seeds. Slice into strips; then cut crosswise to dice.

Heat oil in a large skillet on medium. Sauté onion and pepper over medium heat for about 5 minutes or until onion is transparent. Dice reserved pork roast. Add chili powder, tomatoes, tomato sauce, reserved pork roast, cayenne pepper, and salt. Bring to a boil over high heat; then turn down to low. Cover and simmer for an hour, stirring occasionally. Five minutes before serving, pour beans into a colander and rinse under cold water. Add beans to skillet. Pass Cheddar cheese and hot pepper sauce at the table. Good served with blue corn tortilla chips. Yield: 4 servings

My Family Favorite Pork Roast Three-Day Plan

Day 1: _____ ⤴ **Day 2:** _____

⤴ **Day 3:** _____

Where to find these recipes: _____

_____

_____

(Cookbook title with page #, recipe box, website, etc.)

BEFORE SERVING

Reserve _____ for:

- _____
- _____

Chapter 13: Ham

Ham is the cured leg of pork. A variety of hams are featured in this chapter: deli ham, ham steak, and smoked ham. Allow ¼ - ⅓ pound per person for boneless ham and ⅓ - ½ pound per person for bone-in ham. Some hams are cooked and ready to eat, while others require cooking.

The U.S. Department of Agriculture, (USDA) begins their web page on ham this way:

"Hams: They can be fresh, cook-before-eating, cooked, picnic, and country types. There are so many kinds, and their storage times and cooking times can be quite confusing. This background information serves to carve up the facts and make them easier to understand."

For detailed information, see:
http://www.fsis.usda.gov/Factsheets/Ham/index.asp

Three-Day Plan

Day 1: Grilled Ham & Cheese Sandwiches ⟶ **Day 2:** Chef's Salad ⟶ **Day 3:** Ham & Cheese Omelets

Grilled Ham & Cheese Sandwiches

Approximately 3 tablespoons butter or margarine
8 slices whole-wheat bread
1 pound thinly sliced ham
8 slices American cheese

Soften butter or margarine by grating it into a small bowl. Spread butter or margarine onto one side of bread. Place buttered-side down in dry skillet or griddle (no oil needed). Top with 2 slices of ham and 2 slices cheese. Add top slice of bread, buttered side up, to complete sandwich. Repeat to make 4 sandwiches. Reserve remaining ham for the next two meals. Heat skillet or griddle on medium.

Cook sandwiches for a few minutes, checking frequently, until lightly browned. Carefully turn sandwiches over and cook until lightly browned. Serve warm. Good served with tomato soup. Yield: 4 sandwiches

BEFORE SERVING

Reserve deli ham from Grilled Ham & Cheese Sandwiches for:
- Chef's Salad
- Ham & Cheese Omelets

Chef's Salad

4 eggs
½ teaspoon salt
1 tablespoon vinegar
Half of reserved deli ham from Grilled Ham & Cheese Sandwiches (see previous page)
2 slices Cheddar cheese
2 slices Swiss cheese
1 (10-oz.) package mixed salad greens
Bottled Honey Mustard Salad Dressing
Sunflower seeds
Croutons

First, hard boil eggs. Fill a medium-sized saucepan half full of water. Add salt and vinegar. Bring to a boil over high heat. Turn heat to medium and carefully slide eggs into water using a large spoon. Simmer 18 minutes. Partially cover saucepan with lid and pour off hot water, keeping eggs in the pan. Run cold water over eggs and add ice cubes to cool eggs quickly. Crack and roll eggs; peel. Discard shell and rinse eggs. Cut into fourths. Cut ham, Cheddar cheese, and Swiss cheese into strips. Rinse and dry mixed salad greens in a salad spinner or pat dry with towels. Place greens on 4 plates. Arrange ham and cheeses in a sunburst design, radiating from center. Place hard boil egg wedges at top, bottom, and sides. Pass dressing, sunflower seeds, and croutons at the table. Good served with whole grain crackers. Yield: 4 servings

Ham & Cheese Omelets

4 tablespoons butter or margarine, divided
Half of reserved deli ham from Grilled Ham & Cheese Sandwiches (see page 153)
1 dozen eggs
1 cup grated cheese (Cheddar, Swiss, or American)
Salt and pepper to taste

Preheat oven to 200 degrees F. Using a small (6-inch) sauté pan or skillet, melt 1 tablespoon butter over medium heat. Cut ham into strips. Individual omelets are easier to handle than large omelets. Use 2 or 3 eggs per omelet. Beat eggs. Pour into skillet. Use a spatula to push cooked egg to middle of pan. Lift egg that is cooked to allow uncooked egg to run underneath; gently shake pan back and forth over heat. When eggs are set, add ham and sprinkle on about a ¼ cup cheese, salt and pepper. Pour omelet out of pan onto plate, folding it in half. Keep warm in oven. Repeat to make 4 omelets. Good served with hash-brown potatoes and blueberry muffins. Yield: 4 omelets

Three-Day Plan

Day 1: Ham Steak with Apple Rings ⟶ **Day 2:** Baked Potato Bar ⟶ **Day 3:** Smothered Hash Browns

Ham Steak with Apple Rings

2 tart apples such as Granny Smith
1 tablespoon butter or margarine
1 tablespoon prepared mustard
1 tablespoon water
2 tablespoons brown sugar
¼ teaspoon cinnamon
1 (2-pound) thick-cut, bone-in, fully-cooked ham steak

Rinse, core, and cut apples into rings or slices, leaving skin on. Heat butter or margarine a large skillet on medium-low. Sauté apples for 5 minutes, stirring occasionally. Stir in mustard, water, brown sugar, and cinnamon. Turn down to low, cover, and simmer for 10 minutes. Move apple mixture aside or pour into a bowl. Place ham steak in the skillet and spoon apple mixture on top. Cover and heat on low for about 10 minutes or until ham is warm. Reserve one half of the ham steak for the next two dinners. Divide remaining ham steak into serving-size pieces and place on plates with apples. Spoon juice over ham and apples. Good served with baked sweet potatoes and mashed cauliflower. Yield: 4 servings

> Oven variation:
> Preheat oven to 325 degrees F. Place apples on top of ham steak in 3-quart casserole dish or 9x13x2-inch glass pan. Stir mustard, water, brown sugar, and cinnamon in a small bowl, and pour over apples and ham. Bake for 30 - 45 minutes.

BEFORE SERVING
Reserve half of ham from Ham Steak with Apple Rings for:
- Baked Potato Bar
- Smothered Hash Browns

Baked Potato Bar

8 large baking (white) potatoes
4 eggs
½ teaspoon salt
1 tablespoon vinegar
4 oz. (6 - 8) button mushrooms
1 tablespoon butter or margarine
1 tablespoon oil
Half of reserved ham from Ham Steak with Apple Rings (see previous page)
1 cup grated Cheddar cheese
Butter or margarine
About ½ cup sour cream
Salt and pepper to taste

Preheat oven to 400 degrees F. Scrub potatoes under cold running water. Prick with a fork to allow steam to escape. Bake for an hour or more, until tender, depending on size. Meanwhile, prepare toppings and place in bowls to serve family style.

For hard-boiled eggs, fill a medium-sized saucepan half full of water. Add salt and vinegar. Bring to a boil over high heat. Turn heat to medium and carefully slide eggs into water using a large spoon. Simmer 18 minutes. Partially cover saucepan with lid, and pour off hot water, keeping eggs in the pan. Run cold water over eggs and add ice cubes to cool eggs quickly. Crack and roll eggs; peel. Discard shell and rinse eggs. Dice and place in a serving bowl. Refrigerate until mealtime.

Place mushrooms in a bowl of cool water. Stir with hands; dirt will fall to the bottom of the bowl. To prevent mushrooms from absorbing water, do not let soak. Remove mushrooms from water, and place on a cutting board. Slice about ¼ inch thick. Heat 1 tablespoon butter or margarine and 1 tablespoon oil in a large skillet over medium/medium-high heat. Sauté mushrooms, stirring constantly, for about 3 minutes, until brown and slightly smaller. Pour into a serving bowl. Dice reserved ham and place in a serving bowl.

Before serving, reserve 4 baked potatoes for tomorrow's dinner; refrigerate when cool. To serve: Place hot potatoes on plates. Cut into potato two ways to make a cross (+) in each. Gently press potato to open cross. At the table, pass the butter or margarine, hard-boiled eggs, mushrooms, ham, cheese, sour cream, and salt and pepper to top potatoes. Good served with dinner rolls and butter. Yield: 4 servings

BEFORE SERVING

Reserve 4 baked potatoes from Baked Potato Bar for:
- Smothered Hash Browns

Smothered Hash Browns

1 onion
1 green pepper
4 tablespoons oil, divided
4 large, cold, baked potatoes reserved from Baked Potato Bar (see previous page)
Half of ham reserved from Ham Steak with Apple Rings (see page 156)
1 cup grated Cheddar
Salt and pepper to taste

Using a chef's knife, cut onion in half lengthwise on a cutting board. Peel off outer skin; cut out root end. Place onion flat side down. Score; then cut to dice and chop fine. Rinse green pepper and cut in half. Pull out and discard seeds. Slice into strips; then cut across strips to dice. Heat 2 tablespoons oil on medium in a large, nonstick skillet. Sauté onions and pepper until lightly browned, 5 - 10 minutes. Remove from skillet and set aside.

Grate potatoes into a large bowl. If using a hand grater, the potato skin will act as a covering to help you grip the potato. Discard skin. If using an electric grater, remove skin before grating. Add 2 tablespoons oil to skillet. Add grated potatoes and cook until browned, about 10 minutes. Turn, and continue heating for approximately 10 more minutes. Dice ham. Top potatoes with onions, peppers, ham, and cheese. Heat for a few minutes, just until cheese melts. Sprinkle with salt and pepper. Good served with wheat toast and sliced melon. Yield: 4 servings

Three-Day Plan

Day 1: Brown Sugar Glazed Ham ⤳ **Day 2:** Hearty Ham & Beans ⤳ **Day 3:** Ham & Egg Sandwiches

Brown Sugar Glazed Ham

1 (7-pound) half, bone in, fully-cooked smoked ham
½ cup brown sugar
¼ teaspoon dry mustard
1 teaspoon apple cider vinegar

Place ham in a roasting pan. Bake at 325 degrees F. for 1 ½ hours. For glaze, mix brown sugar, dry mustard and vinegar. Remove ham from oven. Pour off and discard drippings; remove skin. Use a knife to cut a diamond pattern in fat on surface of ham. Pat brown sugar mixture onto scored ham. Place back in oven for 30 minutes (2 hours total cooking time) or until heated through with a meat thermometer reading of 145 degrees F.

Remove ham from oven and let rest for 15 minutes. Carve into slices. Reserve ham bone for the next two recipes. Good served with candied sweet potatoes and roasted asparagus. Yield: 12-16 servings.

Note: start soaking beans for tomorrow's supper.

BEFORE SERVING

Reserve ham bone from Brown Sugar Glazed Ham for:
- Hearty Ham & Beans
- Ham & Egg Sandwiches

AFTER SERVING

Dice remaining ham in 1 - 2-cup servings to use in the following recipes. Refrigerate 2 cups of diced ham for the next 2 recipes, and freeze the rest to use weekly. Note: Ham keeps for 1 - 2 months in the freezer.
- Hearty Ham & Beans
- Ham & Egg Sandwiches
- Ham & Cheese Frittata
- Cheesy Ham & Potato Casserole
- Ham, Egg, & Spinach Salad
- Ham & Swiss Quiche
- Ham & Potato Soup
- Ham & Egg Wraps

Hearty Ham & Beans

1 (1-pound) bag Great Northern beans
Salt and pepper to taste
1 cup diced ham reserved from Brown Sugar Glazed Ham (see previous page)
Ham bone from Brown Sugar Glazed Ham (see previous page)
Bottled hot pepper sauce

Start the day before or use the quick method, below. For overnight method: Pour beans into a bowl and sort through, discarding rocks and dirt. Pour beans into a strainer. Rinse under running water. Pour beans into a large pot. Cover with water two inches higher than the beans. Soak overnight.

For quick method: Pour beans into a bowl and sort through, discarding rocks and dirt. Pour beans into a strainer. Rinse under cold running water. Pour beans into a large pot. Cover with water two inches higher than the beans. Bring to a boil. Boil 2 minutes. Turn off heat and let soak for 1 hour.

Drain soaked or precooked beans with a strainer; rinse under running water. Pour fresh water over beans in a large pot, along with ham bone. (Do not add salt until beans are done.) Bring to a boil and turn down heat to low. Cover and simmer for 1 hour or until soft. Test by tasting or by spooning out a bean and blowing on it. If the skin starts to peel away, it's done. Drain beans.

Remove ham bone from pot. If there's any ham remaining on bone, dice and add to pot, along with 1 cup diced ham. Add salt and pepper to taste. Pass hot pepper sauce at the table. Good served with cornbread. Yield: 6 servings

Ham & Egg Sandwiches

1 tablespoon butter or margarine
6 eggs
6 tablespoons heavy cream OR milk
1 cup diced ham reserved from Brown Sugar Glazed Ham (see page 160)
¼ teaspoon ground black pepper
4 hard rolls

Heat butter or margarine in a large skillet over low heat until melted. Beat eggs in a medium-sized bowl; add cream or milk and ham. Pour egg mixture into skillet and stir until eggs are just cooked. Serve immediately on hard rolls. Good served with potato pancakes and applesauce. Yield: 4 sandwiches

Weekly Plans

Use frozen ham once/week in the following recipes. Defrost in refrigerator the night before, or in the microwave right before cooking.

Week 1: Ham & Cheese Frittata ⟶ **Week 2:** Cheesy Ham & Potato Casserole ⟶ **Week 3:** Ham, Egg, & Spinach Salad ⟶ **Week 4:** Ham & Swiss Quiche ⟶ **Week 5:** Ham & Potato Soup ⟶ **Week 6:** Ham & Egg Wraps

Ham & Cheese Frittata

4 green onions
1 green or red bell pepper
1 small zucchini
2 tablespoons oil
8 eggs
2 cups cubed ham from Brown Sugar Glazed Ham (see page 160)
¼ teaspoon hot pepper sauce
½ teaspoon salt
1 cup grated Cheddar cheese
1 tablespoon chopped fresh parsley
OR 1 teaspoon dried parsley

Preheat oven to 350 degrees F. Grease an 8x8x2-inch glass pan. Rinse green onions. Trim top and root end, and remove loose outer skin. Cut, starting with green top, crosswise into ⅛-inch circles. Rinse green or red pepper and cut in half. Pull out and discard seeds. Slice into approximately ½-inch strips; then cut across strips to dice. Rinse and trim ends of zucchini. Leave skin on. Cut lengthwise into ½-inch slices, then into ½-inch sticks; cut across to dice into ½-inch cubes.

Heat oil in a large skillet on medium. Cook onion, pepper, and zucchini for 3 minutes, stirring occasionally. Meanwhile, beat eggs with a wire whisk in a large bowl. Add ham, pepper sauce, salt, and cheese to eggs. Pour vegetable mixture into prepared baking dish. Pour egg mixture over all. Bake for 35 - 40 minutes or until set.

Meanwhile, place a bunch of fresh parsley in a colander and rinse under cold water. Rub the parsley with your fingers to remove dirt. Shake off excess water. Pat leaves dry with a paper towel. Hold the parsley in a bunch and cut the leaves from the stems. Discard stems. Place leaves in a bowl and snip with kitchen shears or use a knife to chop on a cutting board. Before serving, sprinkle frittata with parsley. Good served with toasted bagels and cream cheese. Yield: 4 servings

Cheesy Ham & Potato Casserole

1 onion
4 tablespoons butter or margarine
1½ cups grated Monterrey Jack cheese
1¼ cups chicken broth
OR 1¼ cups water and 1¼ teaspoons chicken soup base
1 tablespoon cornstarch
1 (8-oz.) carton sour cream
2 cups milk
1 (2-pound) package frozen hash-brown potatoes
2 cups diced ham reserved from Brown Sugar Glazed Ham (see page 160)

Preheat oven to 350 degrees F. Grease a 9x13x2-inch glass baking dish. Using a chef's knife, cut onion in half lengthwise on a cutting board. Peel off outer skin; cut out the root end. Place onion flat side down. Score; then cut to dice. Melt 4 tablespoons butter or margarine in a large skillet over medium heat. Add onion and sauté for 5 minutes or until soft.

Add cheese, broth (or water and soup base), cornstarch, sour cream, and milk. Heat, stirring frequently, until cheese is melted. Pour potatoes and ham into prepared pan. Pour cheese mixture over potatoes and ham. Spread evenly. Bake 1 hour until bubbly and lightly browned. Good served with stir-fried broccoli. Yield: 4-6 servings

Ham, Egg, & Spinach Salad

1 small white onion
¼ cup sugar
3 tablespoons apple cider vinegar, divided
¼ cup oil
3 tablespoons ketchup
½ teaspoon lemon juice
½ teaspoon paprika
1 teaspoon salt, divided
4 eggs
1 (10-oz.) package spinach leaves
2 cups diced ham reserved from Brown Sugar Glazed Ham (see page 160)
1 cup shredded Parmesan cheese
Approximately ¼ cup roasted and salted sunflower nuts
1 cup seasoned croutons

First, make the salad dressing. Trim ends of onion, leaving root end intact; peel off outer skin. Grate onion into a small bowl. Measure 1 tablespoon grated onion and pour into a 1 - 2 cup container with a lid. Add sugar, 2 tablespoons vinegar, oil, ketchup, lemon juice, paprika, and ½ teaspoon salt. Secure lid and shake well (or blend with a fork or small wire whisk). Chill. Meanwhile, prepare salad.

To hard boil eggs, fill a medium-sized saucepan half full of water. Add ½ teaspoon salt and 1 tablespoon vinegar, and bring to a boil over high heat. Turn heat to medium, and carefully slide eggs into water using a large spoon. Simmer 18 minutes. Partially cover with lid and pour off hot water, keeping eggs in the pan. Run cold water over eggs and add ice cubes to cool eggs quickly. Once cool, crack and roll eggs. Peel, discard shell, and rinse eggs. Dice.

Meanwhile, remove stems from spinach; discard stems. Place spinach leaves in a large bowl and add cold water to cover. Use your hand to stir the spinach so dirt and grit can fall to the bottom. Gather the spinach, carrying it up out of the water and into a salad spinner, rotating to dry (or pat dry with towels). Toss spinach and dressing. Serve on plates, and pass bowls family style: egg, ham, cheese, sunflower nuts, and croutons. Good served with multigrain crackers. Yield: 4 servings

Ham & Swiss Quiche

9-inch (1-crust) pie crust:
1½ cups flour
½ teaspoon salt
½ cup shortening, butter or margarine
4-6 tablespoons cold water

Filling:
4 eggs
2 cups light cream
1 cup diced ham reserved from Brown Sugar Glazed Ham (see page 160)
¾ cup Parmesan cheese
1½ cups grated Swiss cheese

> Easy variation: Buy prepared pie dough for a one-crust pie.

For pie dough, measure and mix flour and salt in a medium-sized bowl. Cut in shortening, butter, or margarine with a pastry blender or 2 knives until it resembles meal. Stir in ¼ cup water with a fork. Add additional water, 1 tablespoon at a time, just until dough is mixed and pulls away from the sides. Let dough rest 15 minutes in freezer or 1 hour in refrigerator.

Roll out dough on a floured dishtowel or cutting board. Roll from the center outward into a 12-inch circle about ¼ inch thick. Place in 9-inch pie pan and crimp edges with floured fingers. To crimp, pinch dough with thumb and pointer finger of left hand and press pointer finger from right hand into pinched dough to form a raised edge. Repeat all the way around the rim of the pie.

Cover edge of piecrust with pie shield or strips of aluminum foil. Preheat oven to 350 degrees F. Beat eggs in a large bowl; add cream, ham, and cheeses. Pour filling into crust. Bake 40 minutes, or until set, removing pie shield or aluminum foil 15 minutes before quiche is done. Good served with mixed green salad. Yield: 1 quiche; 4 - 6 servings

Ham & Potato Soup

1 onion
4 medium-sized red potatoes
1 tablespoon oil
1 tablespoon butter or margarine
2 tablespoons flour
2 cups chicken broth
OR 2 cups water and 2 teaspoons chicken soup base
1 cup light cream or milk
1 cup diced ham reserved from Brown Sugar Glazed Ham (see page 160)
Salt and pepper to taste
1 tablespoon chopped fresh parsley
OR 1 teaspoon dried parsley

Using a chef's knife, cut onion in half lengthwise on a cutting board. Peel off outer skin; cut out the root end. Place onion flat side down. Score; then cut to dice and chop fine. Pare and dice potatoes.

Heat oil and butter or margarine in a medium-sized (3-quart) pot on medium. Sauté onion for 5 minutes or until soft. Add flour, stirring until smooth and bubbly. Add potatoes and broth (or water and soup base). Bring to a boil over high heat, stirring occasionally, until thickened and bubbly. Turn down to low, cover, and simmer about 15 minutes or until potatoes are soft. Stir in cream or milk and ham. Heat a few minutes more. Add salt and pepper to taste.

For fresh parsley, place a small bunch in a colander and rinse under cold water. Rub the parsley with your fingers to remove dirt. Shake off excess water. Pat dry with a paper towel. Hold the parsley in a bunch and cut the leaves from the stems. Discard stems. Place leaves in a bowl and snip with kitchen shears or use a knife to chop on a cutting board. Measure and add parsley to soup. Good served with croissants. Yield: 4 servings

Ham & Egg Wraps

20 frozen, seasoned, shredded potato puffs, like Tator Tots ®
8 eggs
1 tablespoon butter or margarine
1 cup diced ham reserved from Brown Sugar Glazed Ham (see page 160)
4 large (burrito-size) flour tortillas
1 cup grated Cheddar cheese
Bottled salsa

Bake potato puffs according to package directions. Meanwhile, break eggs into a large bowl and beat with a wire whisk. Melt butter or margarine in a large skillet over medium heat. Add eggs and ham and stir constantly until eggs are cooked. Heat flour tortillas according to package directions or in the microwave between damp paper towels. Assemble burrito by spooning a fourth of the egg/ham scramble on each tortilla. Top with 5 potato puffs, ¼ cup cheese, and a spoonful of salsa. Fold bottom edge up to keep filling in, roll from left to right. Good served with orange and banana slices. Yield: 4 burritos

My Family Favorite Ham Three-Day Plan

Day 1: _____ ↗ **Day 2:** _____

↗ **Day 3:** _____

Where to find these recipes: _____

_____

_____

(*Cookbook title with page #, recipe box, website, etc.*)

BEFORE SERVING

Reserve _____ for:

- _____

- _____

Delicious Dinners with Fish and Seafood

Two-Day Plan

The U.S. Food and Drug Administration (FDA) states that fish and seafood are safe to keep in the refrigerator for 2 days. So this section follows a 2-day schedule rather than the 3-day schedule in the chicken, turkey, beef, and pork sections.

Defrosting

If fish or seafood is frozen, defrost until pliable before you begin cooking. The best way to defrost fish or seafood is in the refrigerator where it takes about a day. If you defrost fish or seafood on the counter, seal it in a plastic bag, submerge in a bowl of cold water, and check every half hour. If the water is not cold, dump, and add cold water to the bowl. Defrosting fish or seafood in the microwave is a third option. Once the fish or seafood is pliable, but not necessarily completely defrosted, cook it right away.

For more on information about fish and seafood, see the U.S. Food and Drug Administraion (FDA) link:
http://www.fda.gov/Food/ResourcesForYou/Consumers/ucm077331.htm

Chapter 14: Fish and Seafood

Two-Day Plan
Day 1: Tuna Salad Wraps ⟶ **Day 2:** Mediterranean Tuna Salad

Tuna Salad Wraps

3 eggs
¾ teaspoon salt, divided
2 tablespoons cider vinegar, divided
2 (12-oz.) cans tuna
3 ribs celery
4 small sweet pickles
Dash pepper
1 lemon
½ cup mayonnaise
4 burrito-size, whole-wheat flour tortillas
4 large lettuce leaves
2 tomatoes

To hard boil eggs, fill a medium-sized saucepan half full of water. Add ½ teaspoon salt and 1 tablespoon vinegar and bring to a boil over high heat. Turn heat to medium, and carefully slide eggs into water using a large spoon. Simmer 18 minutes. Partially cover with saucepan lid and pour off hot water, keeping eggs in the pan. Run cold water over eggs and add ice cubes to cool eggs quickly. Once cool, crack and roll eggs. Peel, discard shell, and rinse eggs. Dice and pour into a mixing bowl.

Rinse and trim ends and leaves of celery; cut in half crosswise. Cut lengthwise into sticks, then crosswise to dice. Cut pickles in half lengthwise; then cut each half lengthwise into thin slices. Cut crosswise to mince. Add celery and pickles to mixing bowl. Drain tuna; add to bowl. Add ¼ teaspoon salt and a dash of pepper. Cut and squeeze lemon into a separate, small bowl. Stick a fork in the lemon half and rub fork back and forth to squeeze as much juice as possible. Discard seeds and lemon rind. Add juice to bowl, along with mayonnaise; stir to combine. Reserve half of tuna salad for the next dinner.

Rinse and spin lettuce in a salad spinner, or pat dry with paper towels. Rinse and core tomatoes and trim ends. Cut tomatoes into slices; then dice. Place flour tortilla on each plate. Place a lettuce leaf on each tortilla. Spoon tuna salad onto tortillas. Sprinkle with diced tomato. Fold up bottom edge to keep filling in, and roll from left to right. Good served with fresh vegetables and creamy dip: baby carrots, broccoli florets, green bell pepper strips. Yield: 4 servings

BEFORE SERVING

Reserve half of tuna salad for:
- Mediterranean Tuna Salad

Mediterranean Tuna Salad

8-oz. package curly noodles
1 green pepper
1 small (3.8-oz) can sliced black olives
1 cup cubed mozzarella cheese
2 tablespoons Parmesan cheese
Tuna salad reserved from Tuna Salad Wraps (see page 171)
Bottled Italian salad dressing

Cook noodles according to package directions. Drain and rinse under cold water. Rinse and cut green pepper in half. Pull out and discard seeds. Slice into strips; then cut across strips to dice. Mix noodles, green pepper, black olives (drained), mozzarella cheese, Parmesan cheese, and tuna salad. Pour on enough salad dressing to moisten; stir to combine. Good served with cucumber salad and Italian garlic bread. Yield: 4 servings

Two-Day Plan

Day 1: Golden Fried Fish ⟶ **Day 2:** Fish Tacos

Golden Fried Fish

2 pounds white fish fillets, such as cod, haddock, or perch
½ cup milk
Salt and pepper
½ cup flour
1 cup white or yellow cornmeal
About ¼ cup butter or margarine
About ¼ cup oil

Tartar Sauce:
½ cup mayonnaise
2 tablespoons pickle relish
1 teaspoon lemon juice

If fillets are long, cut in half crosswise on a cutting board. Place fillets in a 9x13x2-inch glass dish or 3-quart casserole. Pour milk over fillets; flip fish over to distribute milk. To weaken fishy taste, refrigerate milk-covered fish for ½ hour. Remove fillets from milk to a large platter and pat dry with paper towels. Sprinkle fillets with salt and pepper.

Melt butter or margarine in a large skillet on medium. Add oil to equal about ¼ inch deep. Place flour and cornmeal in separate areas on waxed paper or a plate. Dip fillets first in flour and pat to remove excess flour. Then dip back in milk, then in cornmeal. Place in one layer in hot (but not smoking) oil in skillet. Depending on thickness, fry fillets for 5 - 7 minutes or until golden brown. Turn and fry for an additional 5 - 7 minutes. Only turn once. Fillets 1 inch at the thickest part should cook in 10 minutes total. Fish will turn from translucent to opaque or white and will flake easily when cooked through.

Repeat with remaining fillets. Add more butter or margarine and oil if needed. Reserve a fourth of the fillets for tomorrow's meal. For tartar sauce, mix mayonnaise, pickle relish, and lemon juice in a serving bowl to pass at the table. Good served with baked French fries, coleslaw, hush puppies, and lemon wedges. Yield: 4 servings

BEFORE SERVING
Reserve a fourth of fried fillets for:
- Fish Tacos

Fish Tacos

1 head iceberg lettuce
OR 1 (8-oz.) bag shredded iceberg lettuce
Fried fish fillets reserved from Golden Fried Fish (see previous page)
1 lime
1 red onion
1 (8 - 12 count) package hard or soft taco shells
12-oz. carton sour cream
Bottled taco sauce
Bottled hot pepper sauce

It's best to wash head lettuce a few hours or the night before using to allow for drainage. To wash lettuce, cut out core or rap core on counter hard enough to break it loose. Discard core. Turn lettuce head upside down and run under cold , allowing the water to push apart leaves and flow into the lettuce head. Turn core side down and place in a colander to drain. Store in the refrigerator wrapped in a tea towel or paper towels and a container or plastic bag to continue draining. Once lettuce is drained, shred with a serrated knife by cutting ¼-inch slices.

Preheat oven to 350 degrees F. Place fish fillets on a cookie sheet. Bake for 10 minutes. Cut a lime in half and squeeze juice into a small bowl. Stick a fork in the lime half and rub fork back and forth to squeeze as much juice as possible. Strain or remove seeds with a spoon. Pour lime juice over fish.

Using a chef's knife, cut onion in half lengthwise on a cutting board. Peel off outer skin; cut out the root end. Place onion flat side down. Score; then cut to dice. Heat hard or soft taco shells according to package directions. Flake fish with a fork. Spoon fish into taco shells. Top with onion, lettuce, sour cream, taco sauce and hot pepper sauce. Good served with a citrus salad. Yield: 4 servings

Two-Day Plan
Day 1: Perfect Salmon Bake ⟶ **Day 2:** Salmon Spread

Perfect Salmon Bake
2 pounds of salmon fillets
Approximately 2 tablespoons mayonnaise
Salt and pepper to taste
1 small onion
1 lemon
½ cup chicken broth
OR ½ cup water and ½ teaspoon chicken soup base

Preheat oven to 350 degrees F. Grease a 9x13x2-inch glass baking dish. Place salmon fillets in baking dish. Spread a thin layer of mayonnaise on the fillets using a butter knife or spatula. Sprinkle lightly with salt and pepper. Using a chef's knife, cut onion in half on a cutting board. Peel off outer skin; cut out the root end. Cut onion into thin slices. Spread onion slices on top of fish. Cut lemon in half and remove seeds with a fork. Squeeze fresh lemon over all. Pour broth around salmon. Cover and bake 20 - 30 minutes, depending on thickness, or until salmon flakes. Reserve 1 salmon fillet for the next meal.

Optional: Remove about ¼ of the onion slices and reserve them for the next meal. (Onions will be crunchy—they flavored the salmon and can be discarded, or if you want to serve them, sauté in a skillet in 1 tablespoon oil over medium heat for 5 - 10 minutes.) Good served with roasted potatoes and Brussels Sprouts. Yield: 4 servings

BEFORE SERVING
Reserve 1 salmon fillet and about ¼ of the onion slices for:
- Salmon Spread

Salmon Spread

1 cooked salmon fillet reserved from Perfect Salmon Bake (see previous page)
1 (8-oz.) package cream cheese, softened
Optional: onion slices reserved from Perfect Salmon Bake (see previous page)
1 tablespoon lemon juice
½ teaspoon horseradish
Salt to taste
1 small bunch chives

Start the night before or a few hours before serving as the spread is best served cold. Let cream cheese soften at room temperature for an hour before starting, or place in microwave for 1 minute on a low power level. If you are using onion, chop slices fine.

Place the salmon in a large mixing bowl. Using a fork, flake the salmon. Add cream cheese, onion, lemon juice, and horseradish; stir until well-mixed. Add salt to taste. Chill 2 hours or overnight. Rinse chives and gently dry with a paper towel. Snip with kitchen scissors or chop with a chef's knife on a cutting board. Sprinkle chives over salmon spread. Good served on crackers with orzo salad. Yield: 4 - 6 servings

Two-Day Plan:
Day 1: Lemon Grilled Salmon ⟶ **Day 2:** Salmon Sliders

Lemon Grilled Salmon

1 tablespoon chopped fresh parsley
OR 1 teaspoon dried parsley
⅓ cup butter or margarine
2 lemons
2 tablespoons lemon juice
About 2 tablespoons oil
1½ pounds salmon fillets

For fresh parsley, place a small bunch in a colander and rinse under cold water. Rub the parsley with your fingers to remove dirt. Shake off excess water. Pat dry with a paper towel. Hold the parsley in a bunch and cut the leaves from the stems. Discard stems. Place leaves in a bowl and snip with kitchen shears or use a knife to chop on a cutting board. Set aside.

Melt butter or margarine in a small (1-quart) saucepan. Cut and squeeze 1 lemon into a small bowl. Stick a fork in the lemon half and rub fork back and forth to squeeze as much juice as possible. Remove seeds. Add lemon juice and parsley to saucepan. Cut remaining lemon into wedges and set aside.

Fire up coals or gas grill to medium heat. To help prevent sticking, brush salmon fillets with oil before placing on grill, skinless side down. (Do not move fillets until ready to turn over.) Baste salmon with butter mixture and close the grill lid. In 6 - 8 minutes, carefully lift salmon with a metal spatula and turn over. Baste with butter mixture, close lid, and grill an additional 6 - 8 minutes, depending thickness, or until salmon is opaque. Reserve about a third of the salmon for tomorrow's meal. Good served with lemon wedges, cous cous, and honeyed carrots. Yield: 4 servings

BEFORE SERVING
Reserve a third of the salmon (½ pound) for:
- Salmon Sliders

Salmon Sliders

⅓ of salmon reserved from Lemon Grilled Salmon (see previous page)
20 whole-wheat (or regular) saltine crackers
1 onion
1 egg
⅓ cup mayonnaise
1 tablespoon pickle relish
¼ teaspoon pepper
About 3 tablespoons oil, divided
8 - 12 dinner rolls
1 tablespoon butter or margarine, approximately
2 tomatoes
8 - 12 lettuce leaves

Use a fork to flake salmon in a large bowl. Place crackers in a plastic bag. Crush with a rolling pin. Grate onion. Add cracker crumbs, onion, egg, mayonnaise, pickle relish, and pepper to salmon. Heat about 2 tablespoons oil in a large skillet on medium. Shape into small (2-inch) patties. Cook patties for 3 - 5 minutes or until browned; flip over. Add about 1 tablespoon oil. Cook 3 - 5 additional minutes.

Rinse, core, and trim end of tomatoes. Cut into slices. Rinse and dry lettuce in salad spinner or with towel. Toast rolls and spread with butter or margarine. Place salmon sliders on rolls. Top sliders with tomato slice and lettuce leaf (cut or tear lettuce leaves to size if needed). Good served with broccoli and cheese sauce. Yield: 4 servings

Two-Day Plan

Day 1: Shrimp & Parmesan Pasta ⟶ **Day 2:** Shrimp Creole

Shrimp & Parmesan Pasta

2 pounds fresh shrimp
1 teaspoon salt
1 (8-oz.) package wide egg noodles
2 cloves garlic
4 tablespoons oil
2 teaspoons lemon-pepper seasoning
½ cup grated Parmesan cheese

First, peel shrimp: peel back shell, hold onto tail and gently pull. Carefully remove the vein with a toothpick or under running water. Fill a large (4-quart) pot half full with water; add salt. Heat to boiling over high heat. Add shrimp and return to boil; turn down heat and simmer for 1 - 3 minutes (depending on size of shrimp) until shrimp turns pink. Drain. Reserve half of shrimp for tomorrow's dinner.

Boil pasta according to package directions; drain. Press the flat side of a chef's knife on each garlic clove to break skin. Peel off skin. Trim off root end. Score; then cut to mince. Heat oil in a large skillet on medium. Add garlic and lemon-pepper seasoning, and sauté for 1 minute. Add pasta, Parmesan cheese, and (half of) shrimp to skillet. Stir to combine. Good served with creamed spinach. Yield: 4 servings

BEFORE SERVING

Reserve half of shrimp from Shrimp & Parmesan Pasta for:
- Shrimp Creole

Shrimp Creole

1 onion
1 green pepper
1 rib celery
2 tablespoons oil
2 cloves garlic
¼ cup chopped fresh parsley
OR 1 tablespoon dried parsley
2 bay leaves
½ teaspoon thyme
2 (14½-oz.) cans diced tomatoes
¼ teaspoon salt
⅛ teaspoon sugar
1 tablespoon cornstarch
¼ cup water
½ teaspoon hot pepper sauce
Shrimp reserved from Shrimp & Parmesan Pasta (see previous page)

Using a chef's knife, cut onion in half on a cutting board. Peel off outer skin; cut out the root end. Cut onion into thin slices. Rinse and cut green pepper in half. Pull out and discard seeds. Slice into strips. Rinse and trim ends and leaves of celery; cut in half crosswise. Cut lengthwise into sticks, then crosswise to dice. Heat oil in large skillet on medium. Add onion, pepper, and celery. Sauté about 5 minutes or until crisp-tender. Press the flat side of a chef's knife on garlic clove to break skin. Peel off skin. Trim off root end. Score; then cut to mince. Add garlic to skillet and sauté 1 minute more.

Place a big bunch fresh parsley in a colander and rinse under cold water. Rub the parsley with your fingers to remove dirt. Shake off excess water. Pat dry with a paper towel. Hold the parsley in a bunch and cut the leaves from the stems. Discard stems. Place leaves in a bowl and snip with kitchen shears or use a knife to chop on a cutting board.

Add parsley, bay leaves, thyme, tomatoes, salt, and sugar to tomato mixture. Bring to a boil over high heat; then turn down to low, cover, and simmer 15 minutes. Combine cornstarch, water, and pepper sauce; stir with a fork. Add to skillet, stir and simmer until mixture thickens slightly. Remove bay leaves. Add shrimp to skillet and serve immediately. Good served over rice. Yield: 4 servings

My Family Favorite Fish & Seafood Two-Day Plan

Day 1: _____ ⟶ **Day 2:** _____

Where to find these recipes: _____

_____

(Cookbook title with page #, recipe box, website, etc.)

BEFORE SERVING

Reserve _____ for:

♦ _____

Delicious Meatless Dinners

Two-Day Plan

While it's safe to keep most meatless dishes for more than 2 days in the refrigerator, the meatless chapter follows a 2-day schedule.

Included in this chapter are filling dishes featuring vegetables, cheese, pasta, and rice. It's important to include protein-rich foods such as cheese, nuts, and beans when eating vegetarian meals. Even though I'm not a vegetarian, I like to include meatless meals in my menu plan. Not only are they healthy and low in cost, they are delicious, too.

For more on information about vegetarian nutrition, visit this United States Department of Agriculture (USDA) link: http://www.choosemyplate.gov/healthy-eating-tips/tips-for-vegetarian.html

Chapter 15: Meatless Soups, Stews, and Casseroles

Two-Day Plan

Day 1: Pepper 'n Cheese Dip ⟶ **Day 2:** Chicago Spaghetti

Pepper 'n Cheese Dip

1 (15-oz.) can stewed, diced tomatoes
1 (4-oz.) can diced chili peppers
1 (16-oz.) package American cheese
½ teaspoon cayenne pepper
1 (16-oz.) package tortilla chips

Pour tomatoes and juice into a medium-sized (2-quart) saucepan. Add peppers. Dice cheese and mix with tomatoes and peppers. Heat on medium-low until cheese is melted, stirring frequently. Reserve half of Pepper 'n Cheese Dip for tomorrow's supper. Serve with tortilla chips. Good served with fried potatoes and bean dip. Yield: 4 servings

BEFORE SERVING
Reserve half of Pepper 'n Cheese Dip for:
- Chicago Spaghetti

Chicago Spaghetti

1 (12-oz.) package whole-wheat spaghetti
1 (16-oz.) can spaghetti sauce
Reserved cheese dip from Pepper 'n Cheese Dip (see previous page)

Cook spaghetti according to package directions; drain. Meanwhile, heat spaghetti sauce and cheese dip separately. Spoon spaghetti sauce over spaghetti; top with cheese dip. Good served with a mixed green salad. Yield: 4 servings

---

Two-Day Plan
Day 1: Tasty Tomato Soup ⟶ **Day 2:** Spicy Corn Stew

Tasty Tomato Soup

1 small onion
3 tablespoons butter or margarine
3 tablespoons flour
3 cups vegetable broth
OR 3 cups water and 3 teaspoons vegetable soup base
3 cups tomato juice
1½ teaspoons sugar
¾ teaspoon salt
Pinch pepper

Trim ends of onion, keeping onion whole. Peel off outer skin. Grate onion into a bowl. Melt butter or margarine in a large (4-quart) pot over medium-low heat. Add onion and sauté for 5 - 10 minutes or until translucent. Stir in flour. Add broth (or water and soup base), tomato juice, sugar, salt, and pepper. Bring to a boil. Turn down heat to low. Cover and simmer 20 minutes. Reserve 2 cups of soup for tomorrow's dinner. Good served with grilled cheese sandwiches. Yield: 4 servings

BEFORE SERVING

Reserve 2 cups of soup from Tasty Tomato Soup for:
- Spicy Corn Stew

Spicy Corn Stew

1 onion
1 green bell pepper
1 (16-oz.) bag frozen corn
OR 2 cups fresh corn niblets, cut off the cob
Tomato soup reserved from Tasty Tomato Soup (see previous page)
1 (16-oz.) can diced tomatoes
¼ teaspoon cayenne pepper
Salt and pepper to taste

Use a chef's knife to cut onion in half lengthwise on a cutting board. Peel off outer skin; cut out the root end. Place onion flat side down. Score; then cut to dice. Rinse and cut green pepper in half on a cutting board. Pull out and discard seeds. Slice into strips; then cut across strips to dice. Sauté onion and pepper in a large (4-quart) pot on medium for 5 - 10 minutes or until onion is translucent. Add corn, tomato soup, and diced tomatoes to pot. Heat on high to boiling; then turn down to low and simmer about 20 minutes, until corn is cooked. Add salt and pepper to taste. Good served with multigrain crackers. Yield: 4 servings

Two-Day Plan
Day 1: Ratatouille ⟶ **Day 2:** Spaghetti Supreme

Ratatouille

2 small zucchini
1 eggplant
Salt
1 onion
1 green pepper
1 clove garlic
3 tablespoons oil, divided
4 oz. (6 - 8 medium) button mushrooms
1 (16-oz.) can diced tomatoes
Salt and pepper to taste

Use a chef's knife to rinse and trim ends of zucchini on a cutting board. Leave skin on. Cut lengthwise into approximately ½-inch slices. Cut slices into ½-inch strips. Cut across strips to make ½-inch cubes. Rinse and trim ends of eggplant. Pare eggplant and discard skin. Cut eggplant lengthwise into approximately ½-inch slices. Cut slices into ½-inch strips. Cut across strips to make ½-inch cubes. Shake salt shaker over eggplant and zucchini; toss. The salt will make the zucchini and eggplant sweat, creating a better texture when cooked. Let rest about 30 minutes while preparing the following ingredients.

Meanwhile, cut onion in half and peel off outer skin. Cut out the root end. Score and dice. Rinse and cut green pepper in half. Pull out and discard seeds. Slice into strips; then cut crosswise to dice. Press the flat side of a chef's knife on garlic clove to break skin. Peel off skin. Trim off root end. Score; then cut to mince. Place mushrooms in a bowl of cool water. Stir with hands; dirt will fall to the bottom of the bowl. Remove mushrooms from water; to prevent them from absorbing water, do not let mushrooms soak. Slice about ¼ inch thick.

Heat 1 tablespoon oil in a large skillet on medium/medium-high. Sauté mushrooms, stirring frequently, for 2 minutes. Remove from pan and reserve. Turn down heat to medium and add 2 tablespoons oil. Add onion and pepper. Sauté about 5 minutes or until crisp-tender. Add garlic and sauté 1 minute more.

Add tomatoes and juice. Using a colander, rinse and drain zucchini and eggplant; pat dry with paper towels. Add to skillet along with mushrooms (drained). Turn up heat to high and bring to a boil. Cover and simmer on low about 30 minutes or until eggplant is tender. Taste; add salt and pepper if needed. Reserve half of the mixture for the next meal. Good served with French bread and Brie cheese. Yield: 4 servings

BEFORE SERVING
Reserve half of Ratatouille for:
- Spaghetti Supreme

Spaghetti Supreme

Reserved Ratatouille (see previous page)
1 (16-oz.) can pasta sauce
1 (12-oz.) package thin spaghetti
Grated Parmesan cheese

Add spaghetti sauce to Ratatouille. Warm on low. Prepare pasta according to package directions; drain pasta and rinse. Serve sauce over spaghetti. Pass Parmesan cheese at the table. Good served with black bean and corn salad. Yield: 4 servings

Two-Day Plan

Day 1: Broccoli-Cheese Soup with Potatoes ⟶ **Day 2:** Cheesy Broccoli-Rice Casserole

Broccoli Cheese Soup with Potatoes

4 cups vegetable broth
OR 4 cups water plus 4 teaspoons vegetable soup base
2 medium-sized red potatoes
1 (16-oz.) bag frozen broccoli
2 cups water
2 tablespoons cornstarch
1 (16-oz.) package American cheese

Pour broth (or water and soup base) into a large (4-quart) pot. Meanwhile, pare and rinse potatoes. Using a cutting board, cut into ½-inch slices, then into ½-inch strips, and cut crosswise to dice. Add potatoes to broth. Heat to a boil over high heat, turn down heat to low, and simmer for about 5 minutes. Add broccoli and simmer an additional 5 minutes. Stir together water and cornstarch. Add to pot while stirring. Cut or tear cheese into strips and add to pot. Stir until cheese has melted. Reserve half of soup for the next recipe. Ladle into bowls. Good served with tabouli salad. Yield: 4 servings

BEFORE SERVING

Reserve half of Broccoli-Cheese Soup with Potatoes for:
- Cheesy Broccoli-Rice Casserole

Cheesy Broccoli-Rice Casserole

1 cup brown rice
1 (10-oz.) package frozen chopped broccoli
Reserved Broccoli-Cheese Soup with Potatoes (see previous page)

Cook rice according to package directions. Defrost broccoli in microwave or on stovetop in boiling water; drain. Preheat oven to 350 degrees F. Combine cooked rice, broccoli, and the reserved Broccoli Cheese Soup with Potatoes. Grease a 1½-quart casserole or 8x8x2-inch glass pan. Pour in rice mixture. Bake for about 40 minutes or until hot and bubbly. Good served with whole-wheat crackers, nut butter, and apple slices. Yield: 4 servings

My Family Favorite Meatless Two-Day Plan

Day 1: _____ ⤳ **Day 2:** _____

Where to find these recipes: _____

_____

(*Cookbook title with page #, recipe box, website, etc.*)

BEFORE SERVING

Reserve _____ for:

♦ _____

Two-Day, Three-Day, and Weekly Plans

Day 1: Asian Chicken Salad ⟶ **Day 2:** Creamy Chicken Alfredo ⟶ **Day 3:** Rainy Day Chicken-Rice Soup

Day 1: Chicken Caesar Sandwiches ⟶ **Day 2:** Italian Chicken Spaghetti ⟶ **Day 3:** Chicken Ranch Wraps

Day 1: Spicy Chicken Picante ⟶ **Day 2:** Chicken & Barley Chili ⟶ **Day 3:** Cheesy Chicken Enchiladas

Day 1: Grilled Honey-Lime Chicken ⟶ **Day 2:** Chicken Fajitas ⟶ **Day 3:** Chicken and Walnut Stir-Fry

Day 1: Lemon Chicken ⟶ **Day 2:** California Salad ⟶ **Day 3:** Nine-Mile-High Tostadas

Day 1: Mom's Chicken Noodle Soup ⟶ **Day 2:** Old-Fashioned Chicken Salad ⟶ **Day 3:** Homemade Chicken Pot Pie

Day 1: Spanish-Style Chicken ⟶ **Day 2:** Cheesy Chicken Quesadillas ⟶ **Day 3:** Brunswick Stew

Day 1: Herb-Roasted Chicken ⟶ **Day 2:** Chicken Salad with Sugar-Glazed Pecans ⟶ **Day 3:** Jambalaya

Day 1: Chicken 'n Dumplings ⟶ **Day 2:** Everybody's Favorite Chicken Pasta Salad ⟶ **Day 3:** BBQ Chicken Sandwiches

Day 1: Basic Roast Turkey ⟶ **Day 2:** Hot Turkey Sandwiches with Gravy ⟶ **Day 3:** Homemade Turkey Soup with Pasta

Week 1: Turkey Tetrazzini ⟶ **Week 2:** Turkey 'n Corn Chili ⟶ **Week 3:** Turkey à La King ⟶ **Week 4:** Deep-Dish Turkey with Almonds ⟶ **Week 5:** Turkey Salad Wraps ⟶ **Week 6:** Creamy Turkey Noodle Casserole

Day 1: Herbed Turkey Meatloaf ⟶ **Day 2:** Hearty Turkey-Vegetable Soup ⟶ **Day 3:** Easy Macaroni Skillet Dinner

Day 1: Two-Meat Burritos ⟶ **Day 2:** Italian Pasta Skillet Dinner ⟶ **Day 3:** Spicy Tamale Pie

Day 1: Betty's Spaghetti ⟶ **Day 2:** Quick 'n Easy Chili ⟶ **Day 3:** Kids' Fave Chili-Mac

Day 1: Summer Day Cheeseburgers ⟶ **Day 2:** Cheeseburger Soup ⟶ **Day 3:** Stacked Enchiladas con Huevos

Day 1: Crispy Tacos ⟶ **Day 2:** Beef-Barley Soup ⟶ **Day 3:** Kids' Choice Sloppy Joes

Day 1: Salisbury Steak with Mushroom Sauce ⟶ **Day 2:** Super Nachos ⟶ **Day 3**: Hearty Corn Stew

Day 1: Pizza Rounds ⟶ **Day 2:** Oodles of Noodles Casserole ⟶ **Day 3:** Kansas City Steak Soup

Day 1: Mexican Lasagna ⟶ **Day 2:** Grandma Lil's Stuffed Cabbage ⟶ **Day 3:** Main Dish Taco Salad

Day 1: Meatball Heroes ⟶ **Day 2:** Easy Lasagna ⟶ **Day 3:** Meatball Stew

Day 1: Classic Beef Stew with Wine ⟶ **Day 2:** Shepherd's Pie ⟶ **Day 3:** Quick & Easy Beef and Noodles

Day 1: Steak Supreme ⟶ **Day 2:** Steak and Tomato Salad ⟶ **Day 3:** Steak Fajitas

Day 1: Asian Pepper Steak ⟶ **Day 2:** Spicy Steak & Eggs ⟶ **Day 3:** Philly Cheese Steak Sandwiches

Day 1: Easy French Dip Sandwiches ⟶ **Day 2:** Beef-Vegetable Soup ⟶ **Day 3:** Homemade Beef Pot Pie

Day 1: Nana's Beef Brisket ⟶ **Day 2:** BBQ Beef Sandwiches ⟶ **Day 3:** Borscht

Day 1: Corned Beef & Cabbage ⟶ **Day 2:** Reuben Sandwiches ⟶ **Day 3:** Corned Beef Hash

Day 1: Breakfast-for-Dinner Casserole ⟶ **Day 2:** Sausage-Mushroom Pizza ⟶ **Day 3:** Biscuits & Sausage Gravy

Day 1: Busy Day Goulash ⟶ **Day 2:** Hot Dog Bean Bake ⟶ **Day 3:** Mac 'n Cheese with Hot Dogs

Day 1: Brats on Buns ⟶ **Day 2:** Lentil Soup with Brats ⟶ **Day 3:** Sausage Stew

Day 1: Favorite Pork Chops ⟶ **Day 2:** Pork Fried Rice ⟶ **Day 3:** Hot & Sour Soup

Day 1: Pulled Pork with Honey-Mustard Sauce ⟶ **Day 2:** BBQ Pork Sandwiches ⟶ **Day 3:** Carnitas Burritos

Day 1: Herbed Pork Loin Roast ⟶ **Day 2:** Emily's Pork Lo Mein ⟶ **Day 3:** Spicy Chili with Pork

Day 1: Grilled Ham & Cheese Sandwiches ⟶ **Day 2:** Chef's Salad ⟶ **Day 3:** Ham & Cheese Omelets

Day 1: Ham Steak with Apple Rings ⟶ **Day 2:** Baked Potato Bar ⟶ **Day 3:** Smothered Hash Browns

Day 1: Brown Sugar Glazed Ham ⟶ **Day 2:** Hearty Ham & Beans ⟶ **Day 3:** Ham & Egg Sandwiches

Week 1: Ham & Cheese Frittata ⟶ **Week 2:** Cheesy Ham & Potato Casserole ⟶ **Week 3:** Ham, Egg, & Spinach Salad ⟶ **Week 4:** Ham & Swiss Quiche ⟶ **Week 5:** Ham & Potato Soup ⟶ **Week 6:** Ham & Egg Wraps

Day 1: Tuna Salad Wraps ⟶ **Day 2:** Mediterranean Tuna Salad

Day 1: Golden Fried Fish ⟶ **Day 2:** Fish Tacos

Day 1: Perfect Salmon Bake ⟶ **Day 2:** Salmon Spread

Day 1: Lemon Grilled Salmon ⟶ **Day 2:** Salmon Sliders

Day 1: Shrimp & Parmesan Pasta ⟶ **Day 2:** Shrimp Creole

Day 1: Pepper 'n Cheese Dip ⟶ **Day 2:** Chicago Spaghetti

Day 1: Tasty Tomato Soup ⟶ **Day 2:** Spicy Corn Stew

Day 1: Ratatouille ⟶ **Day 2:** Spaghetti Supreme

Day 1: Broccoli Cheese Soup with Potatoes ⟶ **Day 2:** Cheesy Broccoli-Rice Casserole

Index

Asian Chicken Salad, 13
Asian Pepper Steak , 108
Baked Potato Bar, 157
Basic Roast Turkey, 51
BBQ Beef Sandwiches, 118
BBQ Chicken Sandwiches, 48
BBQ Pork Sandwiches, 144
Beef-Barley Soup, 82
Beef, Ground
- Beef-Barley Soup, 82
- Betty's Spaghetti, 73
- Cheeseburger Soup, 77
- Crispy Tacos, 80
- Easy Lasagna, 96
- Grandma Lil's Stuffed Cabbage, 92
- Hearty Corn Stew, 87
- Kansas City Steak Soup, 90
- Kids' Fave Chili-Mac, 75
- Kids' Choice Sloppy Joes, 83
- Main Dish Taco Salad, 93
- Meatball Heroes, 95
- Meatball Stew, 97
- Mexican Lasagna, 91
- Oodles of Noodles Casserole, 89
- Pizza Rounds, 88
- Quick 'n Easy Chili, 74
- Salisbury Steak with Mushroom Sauce, 84
- Stacked Enchiladas con Huevos, 78
- Summer Day Cheeseburgers, 76
- Super Nachos, 86

Beef Roast
- BBQ Beef Sandwiches, 118
- Beef-Vegetable Soup, 114
- Borscht, 119

- Corned Beef & Cabbage, 120
- Corned Beef Hash, 122
- Easy French Dip Sandwiches, 112
- Homemade Beef Pot Pie, 115
- Nana's Beef Brisket, 117
- Reuben Sandwiches, 121

Beef Steak
- Asian Pepper Steak, 108
- Philly Cheese Steak Sandwiches, 110
- Spicy Steak & Eggs, 109
- Steak and Tomato Salad, 106
- Steak Fajitas, 107
- Steak Supreme, 104

Beef Stew
- Classic Beef Stew with Wine, 99
- Quick & Easy Beef and Noodles, 102
- Shepherd's Pie, 101

Beef-Vegetable Soup, 114

Betty's Spaghetti, 73

Biscuits & Sausage Gravy, 128

Borscht, 119

Brats on Buns, 132

Bratwurst
- Brats on Buns, 132
- Lentil Soup with Brats, 133
- Sausage Stew, 134

Breakfast-for-Dinner Casserole, 125

Broccoli Cheese Soup with Potatoes, 191

Brown Sugar Glazed Ham, 160

Brunswick Stew, 40

Busy Day Goulash, 129

California Salad, 28

Carnitas Burritos, 146

Casseroles
- Breakfast-for-Dinner Casserole, 125
- Cheesy Broccoli-Rice Casserole, 192
- Cheesy Ham & Potato Casserole, 164

- Creamy Turkey Noodle Casserole, 61
- Deep-Dish Turkey with Almonds, 59
- Oodles of Noodles Casserole, 89

Cheeseburger Soup, 77
Cheesy Broccoli-Rice Casserole, 192
Cheesy Chicken Enchiladas, 23
Cheesy Chicken Quesadillas, 39
Cheesy Ham & Potato Casserole, 164
Chef's Salad, 154
Chicago Spaghetti, 187
Chicken & Barley Chili, 22
Chicken Breasts
- Asian Chicken Salad, 13
- California Salad, 28
- Cheesy Chicken Enchiladas, 23
- Chicken & Barley Chili, 22
- Chicken Caesar Sandwiches, 18
- Chicken Ranch Wraps, 20
- Creamy Chicken Alfredo, 15
- Italian Chicken Spaghetti, 19
- Lemon Chicken, 27
- Nine-Mile-High Tostadas, 30
- Rainy Day Chicken-Rice Soup, 16
- Spicy Chicken Picante, 21

Chicken Caesar Sandwiches, 18
Chicken 'n Dumplings, 45
Chicken Ranch Wraps, 20
Chicken Salad with Sugar-Glazed Pecans, 42
Chicken, Whole
- BBQ Chicken Sandwiches, 48
- Brunswick Stew, 40
- Cheesy Chicken Quesadillas, 39
- Chicken 'n Dumplings, 45
- Chicken Salad with Sugar-Glazed Pecans, 42
- Everybody's Favorite Chicken Pasta Salad, 47
- Herb-Roasted Chicken, 41
- Homemade Chicken Pot Pie, 36

- Jambalaya, 43
- Mom's Chicken Noodle Soup, 34
- Old-Fashioned Chicken Salad, 35
- Spanish-Style Chicken, 38

Classic Beef Stew with Wine, 99
Corned Beef & Cabbage, 120
Corned Beef Hash, 122
Creamy Chicken Alfredo, 15
Creamy Turkey Noodle Casserole, 61
Crispy Tacos, 80
Deep-Dish Turkey with Almonds, 59
Easy French Dip Sandwiches, 112
Easy Lasagna, 96
Easy Macaroni Skillet Dinner, 66
Emily's Pork Lo Mein, 149
Everybody's Favorite Chicken Pasta Salad, 47
Favorite Pork Chops, 137
Fish
- Fish Tacos, 175
- Golden Fried Fish, 174
- Lemon Grilled Salmon, 179
- Mediterranean Tuna Salad, 173
- Perfect Salmon Bake, 177
- Salmon Sliders, 180
- Salmon Spread, 178
- Tuna Salad Wraps, 171

Fish Tacos, 175
Grandma Lil's Stuffed Cabbage, 92
Grilled Ham & Cheese Sandwiches, 153
Ham
- Baked Potato Bar, 157
- Brown Sugar Glazed Ham, 160
- Cheesy Ham & Potato Casserole, 164
- Chef's Salad, 154
- Grilled Ham & Cheese Sandwiches, 153
- Ham & Cheese Frittata, 163
- Ham & Cheese Omelets, 155

- Ham & Egg Sandwiches, 162
- Ham & Egg Wraps, 168
- Ham & Potato Soup, 167
- Ham & Swiss Quiche, 166
- Ham, Egg, & Spinach Salad, 165
- Ham Steak with Apple Rings, 156
- Hearty Ham & Beans, 161
- Smothered Hash Browns, 159

Ham & Cheese Frittata, 163
Ham & Cheese Omelets, 155
Ham & Egg Sandwiches, 162
Ham & Egg Wraps, 168
Ham & Potato Soup, 167
Ham & Swiss Quiche, 166
Ham Steak with Apple Rings, 156
Ham, Egg, & Spinach Salad, 165
Hearty Corn Stew, 87
Hearty Ham & Beans, 161
Hearty Turkey-Vegetable Soup, 65
Herb-Roasted Chicken, 41
Herbed Pork Loin Roast, 148
Herbed Turkey Meatloaf, 64
Homemade Beef Pot Pie, 115
Homemade Chicken Pot Pie, 36
Homemade Turkey Soup with Pasta, 53
Hot & Sour Soup, 140
Hot Dog Bean Bake, 130
Hot Dogs
- Busy Day Goulash, 129
- Hot Dog Bean Bake, 130
- Mac 'n Cheese with Hot Dogs, 131

Hot Turkey Sandwiches with Gravy, 53
Italian Chicken Spaghetti, 19
Italian Pasta Skillet Dinner, 68
Jambalaya, 43
Kansas City Steak Soup, 90
Kids' Choice Sloppy Joes, 83

Kids' Fave Chili-Mac, 75
Lemon Chicken, 27
Lemon Grilled Salmon, 179
Lentil Soup with Brats, 133
Mac 'n Cheese with Hot Dogs, 131
Main Dish Taco Salad, 93
Meatball Heroes, 95
Meatball Stew, 97
Meatless
- Broccoli Cheese Soup with Potatoes, 191
- Cheesy Broccoli-Rice Casserole, 192
- Chicago Spaghetti, 187
- Pepper 'n Cheese Dip, 186
- Ratatouille, 189
- Spaghetti Supreme, 190
- Spicy Corn Stew, 188
- Tasty Tomato Soup, 187

Mediterranean Tuna Salad, 173
Mexican Lasagna, 91
Mom's Chicken Noodle Soup, 34
Nana's Beef Brisket, 117
Nine-Mile-High Tostadas, 30
Old-Fashioned Chicken Salad, 35
Oodles of Noodles Casserole, 89
Pepper 'n Cheese Dip, 186
Perfect Salmon Bake, 177
Philly Cheese Steak Sandwiches, 110
Pie
- Ham & Swiss Quiche, 166
- Homemade Beef Pot Pie, 115
- Homemade Chicken Pot Pie, 36
- Shepherd's Pie, 101
- Spicy Tamale Pie, 69

Pizza Rounds, 88
Pork chops
- Favorite Pork Chops, 137
- Hot & Sour Soup, 140

- Pork Fried Rice, 139

Pork Fried Rice, 139

Pork Roast
- BBQ Pork Sandwiches, 144
- Carnitas Burritos, 146
- Emily's Pork Lo Mein, 149
- Herbed Pork Loin Roast, 148
- Pulled Pork with Honey-Mustard Sauce, 143
- Spicy Chili with Pork, 150

Pork Sausage
- Biscuits & Sausage Gravy, 128
- Breakfast-for-Dinner Casserole, 125
- Sausage-Mushroom Pizza, 126

Pulled Pork with Honey-Mustard Sauce, 143
Quick & Easy Beef and Noodles, 102
Quick 'n Easy Chili, 74
Rainy Day Chicken-Rice Soup, 16
Ratatouille, 189
Reuben Sandwiches, 121
Salads
- Asian Chicken Salad, 13
- California Salad, 28
- Chef's Salad, 154
- Chicken Salad with Sugar-Glazed Pecans, 42
- Everybody's Favorite Chicken Pasta Salad, 47
- Ham, Egg, & Spinach Salad, 165
- Main Dish Taco Salad, 93
- Mediterranean Tuna Salad, 173
- Old-Fashioned Chicken Salad, 35
- Steak and Tomato Salad, 106

Salisbury Steak with Mushroom Sauce, 84
Salmon Sliders, 180
Salmon Spread, 178
Sandwiches
- BBQ Beef Sandwiches, 118
- BBQ Chicken Sandwiches, 48
- BBQ Pork Sandwiches, 144

- Brats on Buns, 132
- Chicken Caesar Sandwiches, 18
- Easy French Dip Sandwiches, 112
- Grilled Ham & Cheese Sandwiches, 153
- Ham & Egg Sandwiches, 162
- Hot Turkey Sandwiches with Gravy, 53
- Kids' Choice Sloppy Joes, 83
- Meatball Heroes, 95
- Philly Cheese Steak Sandwiches, 110
- Reuben Sandwiches, 121
- Salmon Sliders, 180
- Summer Day Cheeseburgers, 76

Sausage-Mushroom Pizza, 126
Sausage Stew, 134
Shepherd's Pie, 101
Shrimp
- Shrimp & Parmesan Pasta, 181
- Shrimp Creole, 182

Shrimp & Parmesan Pasta, 181
Shrimp Creole, 182
Smothered Hash Browns, 159
Soup
- Beef-Barley Soup, 82
- Beef-Vegetable Soup, 114
- Borscht, 119
- Broccoli Cheese Soup with Potatoes, 191
- Cheeseburger Soup, 77
- Chicken & Barley Chili, 22
- Ham & Potato Soup, 167
- Hearty Turkey-Vegetable Soup, 65
- Homemade Turkey Soup with Pasta, 53
- Hot & Sour Soup, 140
- Kansas City Steak Soup, 90
- Lentil Soup with Brats, 133
- Mom's Chicken Noodle Soup, 34
- Quick 'n Easy Chili, 74
- Rainy Day Chicken-Rice Soup, 16

- Spicy Chili with Pork, 150
- Tasty Tomato Soup, 187
- Turkey 'n Corn Chili, 56

Spaghetti Supreme, 190
Spanish-Style Chicken, 38
Spicy Chicken Picante, 21
Spicy Chili with Pork, 150
Spicy Corn Stew, 188
Spicy Steak & Eggs, 109
Spicy Tamale Pie, 69
Stacked Enchiladas con Huevos, 78
Steak and Tomato Salad, 106
Steak Fajitas, 107
Steak Supreme, 104
Stew
- Brunswick Stew, 40
- Busy Day Goulash, 129
- Classic Beef Stew with Wine, 99
- Hearty Corn Stew, 87
- Meatball Stew, 97
- Sausage Stew, 134
- Spicy Corn Stew, 188

Summer Day Cheeseburgers, 76
Super Nachos, 86
Turkey, Ground
- Easy Macaroni Skillet Dinner, 66
- Hearty Turkey-Vegetable Soup, 65
- Herbed Turkey Meatloaf, 64

Turkey, Roast
- Basic Roast Turkey, 51
- Creamy Turkey Noodle Casserole, 61
- Deep-Dish Turkey with Almonds, 59
- Homemade Turkey Soup with Pasta, 53
- Hot Turkey Sandwiches with Gravy, 53
- Turkey à la King, 57
- Turkey 'n Corn Chili, 56
- Turkey Salad Wraps, 60

- Turkey Tetrazzini, 55

Tasty Tomato Soup, 187
Turkey à La King, 57
Turkey/Beef Blend, Ground
- Italian Pasta Skillet Dinner, 68
- Spicy Tamale Pie, 69
- Two-Meat Burritos, 67

Turkey 'n Corn Chili, 56
Turkey Salad Wraps, 60
Turkey Tetrazzini, 55
Two-Meat Burritos, 67
Wraps
- Chicken Ranch Wraps, 20
- Ham & Egg Wraps, 168
- Tuna Salad Wraps, 171
- Turkey Salad Wraps, 60